# Lobby Hero

# KENNETH LONERGAN

# Lobby Hero

Grove Press
New York

*Printed in the United States of America*

ISBN: 978-0-8021-3855-2

Grove Press
an imprint of Grove/Atlantic, Inc.
841 Broadway
New York, NY 10003

Distributed by Publishers Group West

www.groveatlantic.com

13 14 15 16     11 10 9 8 7 6 5 4 3

The world premiere of *Lobby Hero* was produced by Playwrights Horizons, Inc. and opened in New York City on March 13, 2001. Tim Sanford, Artistic Director; Leslie Marcus, Managing Director; William Russo, General Manager. The production was directed by Mark Brokaw; set design by Allen Moyer; costume design by Michael Krass; lighting design by Mark McCullough; sound design by Janet Kalas; and casting by James Calleri. The production manager was Christopher Boll and the production stage manager was James FitzSimmons. The cast was as follows:

| | |
|---|---|
| Jeff | Glenn Fitzgerald |
| William | Dion Graham |
| Dawn | Heather Burns |
| Bill | Tate Donovan |

The Playwrights Horizons production of *Lobby Hero* was subsequently presented Off-Broadway by Jenny Wiener, Jon Steingart and Hal Luftig. It opened at The John Houseman Theater on May 8, 2001.

# CHARACTERS

| | |
|---|---|
| Jeff | a uniformed security guard, late twenties |
| William | his captain, late twenties |
| Bill | a uniformed policeman, around thirty |
| Dawn | his rookie partner, early twenties |

The play takes place in the spacious lobby of a middle-income high-rise apartment building in Manhattan and in the street outside.

# ACT ONE, SCENE ONE

*The spacious, impersonal lobby of a middle-income high-rise apartment building in Manhattan, and the street immediately outside the glass lobby doors. It is very late at night in mid-November. We hear the periodic sound of cars going by. JEFF, a uniformed security guard in his late twenties, is at his station reading a paperback novel. WILLIAM, his uniformed supervisor, black, and also in his late twenties, enters onto the street, then into the lobby.*

**JEFF**  Hey, William.

**WILLIAM**  How's it going there, Jeff?

**JEFF**  Oh, just fine thanks.

**WILLIAM**  Any problems tonight?

**JEFF**  No, none to speak of.

**WILLIAM**  None "to speak of?"

**JEFF**  No problems.

**WILLIAM**  You want to tell me what the police were doing here?

**JEFF**  Oh . . .

**WILLIAM**  That was the police I just saw coming out the building, wasn't it?

**JEFF**  Oh—Yeah. But—

**WILLIAM**  You want to tell me what they were doing here?

**JEFF**  Oh—they were just making a social call, that's all.

**WILLIAM**  On you?

**JEFF**  What?

**WILLIAM**  A social call on you?

**JEFF**  (*Laughs*)  No, on one of the tenants.

**WILLIAM**  Can I see your book?

**JEFF**  Sure.

*William looks at the sign-in book at Jeff's station.*

**WILLIAM**  Is there some reason you didn't write it down?

**JEFF**  Um—

**WILLIAM**  Do you know you're supposed to write it down?

**JEFF**  Um, yeah.

**WILLIAM**  Do you know that whenever the police come to the premises you're supposed to make an entry? That's what this Special Remarks is for, right here.

**JEFF**  Yeah, I—

**WILLIAM**  Did you know that?

**JEFF**  Yes.

**WILLIAM**  Then how come there's no entry?

**JEFF**  Because they were here on a social visit, that's why.

**WILLIAM**  Then how come there's no entry on the sign-in sheet?

**JEFF**  Because I'm a fuck-up?

**WILLIAM**  See? No record in the Special Remarks and nobody signed it in the book. No record. No entry.

**JEFF**  Do you make the cops sign the book?

**WILLIAM**   Yes. Or I sign it for them. Yes. And that's what you do too. That's what everybody does, who works under me. Now—(*Jeff starts to speak.*) No no no, look, if you stick to the rules, then you never have to have a discussion about whether or not you were justified *not* sticking to the rules, you understand? Now next time the cops come, if it's official business, make a special entry. If it's a social visit and you don't wish to offend, then enter the visit yourself. OK?

**JEFF**   OK.

**WILLIAM**   Now write it down. And estimate when they arrived and when they left. (*As Jeff does so*) See, man, it's sloppy. It's sloppy. Every time I come in here, man, you're always laughing and telling jokes and putting on the charm, and you're sloppy on the job. Look at this. Look at this. (*Opens the drawers of Jeff's station*) Look at this mess in here, man. It's—Look at this shit. You got gum wrappers, sandwich bags, pornographic magazines—This is a disgusting mess. Now I want you to clean this shit up, man. Tonight. After you're through with your shift. Because I don't want you cleaning up this refuse while you're on duty, man. That's on your own time.

**JEFF**   Hey William, gimme a break.

**WILLIAM**   No, man—

**JEFF**   I am like the most conscientious guy in this whole building. The rest of these guys are like a bunch of crack addicts and degenerates—

**WILLIAM**   Not for long they're not.

**JEFF**   Not for long? They're a bunch of—

**WILLIAM**   (*On "They're"*)   Any man on my command who can't straighten out and fly right is gonna get busted, man.

I'm giving you guys fair warning, and that means you too, Jeff, man. You're a good man, OK? We're friends and everything. But you're always making jokes.

JEFF (*Starts to protest*) —

WILLIAM  No, listen. Every time I turn around I'm hearing one joke after another and it makes me question how serious a person you are.

JEFF  How else am I supposed to stay awake?

*William is not amused.*

JEFF  I'm just kidding.

WILLIAM  I'm glad to hear that, Jeff, because if I ever catch you or anybody else ever sleeping on a shift I will fire your ass on the spot, just like I did last week with Louie Moore, over on Fifty-eighth street. He was two years away from retirement, I found him asleep on his shift, and I stood him up and I ripped the badge right off his shirt and I'll do the same thing to you. Do you understand me?

JEFF  Yes, yes, I understand. That certainly was terrific how you fired that skinny old man right before he was supposed to retire.

WILLIAM  He wasn't doing his job, man. Nobody's paying him to take a nap. Now I'm gonna ask you again. What were the cops doing here?

JEFF  I *told* you why they were here.

WILLIAM  Because if they were here asking to see me, Jeff, I want you to tell me. Even if they told you not to. I want you to tell me. Do you understand?

JEFF  What? They didn't ask about you.

**WILLIAM**  OK.

**JEFF**  Why would he be looking for you? Or shouldn't I ask.

**WILLIAM**  It's none of your business, man.

**JEFF**  OK. I'm not askin'.

**WILLIAM**  See? Always gotta be invading somebody's private business.

**JEFF**  Hey, get off my *back,* all right?

**WILLIAM**  Excuse me?

**JEFF**  I said get off my back. I didn't *do* anything to you. And this is not even my shit in here, it's Manuel's.

*He slaps the drawer closed.*

**WILLIAM**  All right. I'm sorry. I got a call—my fuckin' brother got picked up by the cops—I don't even want to *tell* you what for—and I just want to be prepared if the police come around asking about his whereabouts.

**JEFF**  Oh. (*Beat*) OK. I'm sorry.

**WILLIAM**  That's all right.

**JEFF**  Well—They really weren't here to see you.

**WILLIAM**  All right. It just seemed like a strange coincidence.

**JEFF**  Well, I mean—is your brother all right?

**WILLIAM**  I don't know. I haven't spoken to him.

**JEFF**  I didn't even know you had a brother.

**WILLIAM**  Well, I do.

**JEFF**  What did they bust him for?

*William shakes his head.*

**JEFF**  OK, skip it.

**WILLIAM**  My brother's fucked up. He's always been a
fuck-up. Always been selfish. Always been wild and selfish:
You know the type. Living like a free spirit or what have
you, while everybody else is trying to work. You know the
type? I mean—I don't know, man. Sometimes you just have
to wash your hands of a person. Because you just get no
recompense. You know what I mean there, Jeff? You must
know what I mean. You've seen something of the world.
I've never seen anything of the world. I've been working
for security firms since I was sixteen years old. Do you
know I'm the youngest captain in the history of this firm?
But I'm square, man. You know? I'm square. I'm no fun.

**JEFF**  That's very true.

**WILLIAM**  And I will bust your ass, all you guys, if you mess
up on my shifts, because I don't *let* people mess up on my
shifts. That's how I got to *be* the youngest captain in the
history of this fucking no-account security firm. I can't
believe some of the people they hire, man. Can you? I
mean—Did you happen to see that article in *The New York
Times* about security companies in New York City? Guys
with long prison records, rapists, murderers, anybody at all
who can sign his name they stick a gun on his waist and set
him up to protect somebody. You want to explain that
insanity to me? I personally got rid of three guys they had
working for this company, man, because these guys were
just out-and-out criminals. You can't just hire anybody who
looks like he can manhandle a person, you know?

**JEFF**  Sure.

**WILLIAM**  Anyway, I'm just rambling.

**JEFF**  Ramble away, man. This is the highlight of my night.

**WILLIAM**  So how's it going with you anyway, Jeff? Everything all right?

**JEFF**  Yeah, pretty good. I been looking for apartments.

**WILLIAM**  Oh yeah? How's that going?

**JEFF**  Pretty good. I saw this one place today that was actually really pretty nice, but it was a little out of my range. I still owe my brother a lot of money.

**WILLIAM**  Maybe he'll forgive the debt.

**JEFF**  I don't want him to forgive the debt. I wanna pay him back every cent I owe him—with interest. The hell with that. I'd rather live in that room for the next five years if it meant I couldn't pay him back. I'm a reformed character, man. I don't take nothin' off of nobody, no thank you, no more.

**WILLIAM**  I can see I've been a very positive influence on you, Jeff.

**JEFF**  You have man, you're a positive inspiration.

*Silence.*

**JEFF**  Hey, you know, I got that book you told me about . . . *The Six Habits of Self-Motivated People*?

**WILLIAM**  Oh yeah? Did you read it?

**JEFF**  Well, I *tried* to read it . . .

**WILLIAM**  All right, you know what?

**JEFF**  —I just couldn't get past the first two habits.

**WILLIAM**  Yeah, all right—

**JEFF** —I guess I wasn't really that motivated.

**WILLIAM** —All right, never mind.

**JEFF** No, seriously. I did try to read it. I just don't usually respond to that kind of stuff. I mean I'm sure it has good stuff in it . . . It just kind of seemed like bullshit to me.

**WILLIAM** Well, you have to have an open mind.

**JEFF** Yeah, I guess . . .

**WILLIAM** And you have to be willing to address some of your own shortcomings. Otherwise you're just wasting your time.

**JEFF** Well, see, I don't have any shortcomings. So that's probably why I couldn't get into it . . .

*William is not amused.*

**JEFF** I do have a terrific sense of humor though. That's one thing you can definitely say about me.

**WILLIAM** Yeah. Keep laughing, Jeff.

**JEFF** I'm just kidding. Maybe it was good. To tell you the truth I couldn't really focus on it too well. I'm having trouble concentrating on anything I read lately.

**WILLIAM** Oh yeah? Why is that?

**JEFF** I don't know. I guess I have a lot on my mind these days.

**WILLIAM** Like what?

**JEFF** Well, my best friend from when I was a kid, my friend Scott, is getting married in a few days, so I've been roped into arranging this bachelor party we're supposed to give him. So that's distracting . . .

8

**WILLIAM**  From what?

**JEFF**  What?

**WILLIAM**  Distracting from what? All you do is sit here. You have no interests—

**JEFF**  I have interests—

**WILLIAM**  No family—

**JEFF**  I have a family—

**WILLIAM**  But you have no wife, no children—

**JEFF**  Oh, well—

**WILLIAM**  That's what *I* mean by a family—Somebody you're responsible for.

**JEFF**  Well—

**WILLIAM**  —You have no ambition, as far as I can see—

**JEFF**  I don't tell you everything about myself.

**WILLIAM**  OK, good. I'm glad to hear it. But that's why I try to get you to improve your mind a little bit and apply yourself to something. Aim a little higher. But I can see it's a hopeless cause.

**JEFF**  You just don't want to admit—

**WILLIAM**  (*Without stopping*)  You're probably intended to be just one of those guys who drifts through life doing one job or another, no plan, no specific intentions of any kind . . . And one day you're gonna wake up in a lobby just like this one, except everybody's gonna be calling you "Pops." And then you're gonna look back and remember: "I should have listened to that guy William. He's the only one that ever took the time to try to encourage me to cultivate

9

my potential. My whole family was content to see me fritter my life away, but that William, man, he really tried to get me to focus my energies a little bit. And doddering useless old unemployed Pops doorman that I am, I have to admit he could have been a positive influence on me if I hadn't been such a callous, careless kind of joke-telling, sit-on-my-ass-my-whole-life type of person when I was younger." But I guess that's all right, because you're not really trying to climb any higher anyway. You see what I mean?

JEFF  I just wish to hell you'd stop trying to butter me up all the time. You know it's embarrassing for both of us the way you're always coming in here trying to kiss my ass.

WILLIAM  OK. Keep laughing, Jeff. 'Cause the joker laughs last. And the joker's gonna laugh last at you.

JEFF  What do you mean, like the Joker from *Batman*?

WILLIAM  No—

JEFF  What the fuck are you talking about?

WILLIAM  I just mean—Like, you know, like the generic joker. Like the laughing figure of Fate, or whatever you want to call it.

JEFF  (*A joke*)  Oh, sure, *that* joker. Everyone's terrified of *him*.

WILLIAM  Go ahead and laugh, Jeff. The joker laughs last.

JEFF  I have interests . . .

WILLIAM  I'm glad to hear it.

JEFF  . . . Just 'cause I don't tell *you* about it doesn't mean I don't have them.

WILLIAM  All right, good.

**JEFF**
—Anyway you work here too, man! So what are you getting on *my* ass about it for? What do you mean, "No you don't"? *You're* working the graveyard shift!

**WILLIAM**
Oh no I don't!

**WILLIAM**  *I'm* working the graveyard shift 'cause that's the shift everybody messes up, OK? I told Joe Collier I was gonna weed out the bad apples in this company and that's exactly what I'm gonna do. That's what I'm doing on the graveyard shift, Jeff. I'm not just sitting here getting old before my time . . .

**JEFF**
I'm not getting old before my time— Oh good for you!

**WILLIAM**
. . . I'm working my way through the ranks . . .

**WILLIAM**  . . . and by the time I'm through I'm gonna clean this place up and move up into management, and if they don't want to move me up the way that I deserve, I'm gonna go off on my own and set myself up to compete with these bums, because I know I could do a better job than them with my eyes closed.

**JEFF**  OK, good for you. *I* was in the Goddamn *Navy* for three years . . .

**WILLIAM**  All right, don't lose your temper . . .

**JEFF**  No, man, why you gotta come in here and be ragging on me all the time?

**WILLIAM**  Oh, oh, you can dish it out but you can't take it.

**JEFF**  I can take it, but there's a *limit*. There's a *level*. I been busting my ass all year tryin' to get my shit together.

**WILLIAM**  All right—

**JEFF**  —You of all people should be *encouraging* me. I just had a little bad luck, that's all. Anybody could have a little bad luck.

**WILLIAM**  Didn't you tell me you got kicked out of the Navy for being on guard duty smoking marijuana?

**JEFF**  Yeah, but it was bad luck that I got *caught*. The rest of my friends are still sailin' the ocean blue gettin' stoned out of their minds. I get high *one time* and suddenly I'm out on my ass?

**WILLIAM**  All I'm sayin' is if you hadn't been smoking that stuff in the first place you wouldn't have to be relying on any kind of luck—good, bad, or otherwise. Personally, I believe in giving people a second chance. And I like you. I don't know why I like you, but I do. I regard you as a project. I think you have a lot of potential.

**JEFF**  No you don't.

**WILLIAM**  Yes I do, Jeff. Because every human being walking around on this earth has potential, Jeff, including you.

**JEFF**  Oh Jesus Christ.

**WILLIAM**  Go ahead and laugh. You probably have more potential than the rest of these guys put together.

*Pause.*

**JEFF**  You think?

**WILLIAM**  Yes I do. If you really applied yourself . . . ? Who knows what you might be good at down the road?

**JEFF**  Well, thanks, William. I take that as encouragement.

**WILLIAM**  That's how it's meant. But you can't just—

**JEFF**  I always thought I had a lot of potential. I guess I just lost my way a little bit.

**WILLIAM**  That happens to a lot of people, Jeff. But you can't just—

**JEFF**  I know. And I'm not blaming anybody else—seriously. But I really had a rough time the last couple of years.

**WILLIAM**  (*Starts to speak*)  —

**JEFF**  I'm not sayin' it's all bad luck. I know you gotta take some responsibility for yourself—

**WILLIAM**  That's right.

**JEFF**  I know, I know. But do you know from the time I came home from the Navy my old man wouldn't even talk to me? I only went into the Navy to get him off my back in the first place. Then I get kicked out—

**WILLIAM**  Why wouldn't he talk to you?

**JEFF**  Because he was ashamed of me, that's why. 'Cause he was this big Navy guy, 'cause he saved all these guys' lives on his ship when he was in Korea. Big deal.

**WILLIAM**  Really.

**JEFF**  Yeah. It's actually a really amazing story. Ship hits an old mine at two o'clock in the morning, twenty-three guys trapped below decks. Everybody jumps overboard except my old man. He finds a blowtorch, goes below decks in the pitch dark, the ship is goin' like *this* (makes a steep incline with his hand), these guys are screamin' for their lives, there's water comin' up to his elbows . . . Two minutes before the ship goes down he cuts open the bulkhead, everybody gets out. Twenty-three guys he saved, not one of 'em drowned.

**WILLIAM**   That's very impressive.

**JEFF**   Yeah: I know: 'Cause my whole *life* I gotta hear this fuckin' story. Several times a year as you can probably imagine, over and over and over again. Every year when I was a kid they had this big get-together in New Jersey; they send flowers, cards, whiskey, cigars, all these old guys and their wives and kids and grandkids cryin' and kissin' my old man and makin' speeches about what a great guy he is. And I'm like, Yeah, that's because you only gotta see the guy *once a year,* for like three and a half hours at a time. Any of you morons tried living with this guy for two days you'd throw him in the fucking ocean and drown him yourself. Asshole. Maybe if *my* ship woulda blown up I woulda got a better start in life. Anyway, so naturally when I got kicked out the guy won't even talk to me. And I don't mean for a few days. I mean he never talked to me again. He don't want my *mother* talking to me, I got nowhere to live, I bum around like a . . . *bum.* I gotta move in with Marty, which is totally humiliating. My old man dies, thank God—

**WILLIAM**   All right . . .

**JEFF**   —I can't get a job, I try to work up a little stake playing poker, I turn around I got the Goddamn loan sharks comin' after me, I gotta borrow five thousand dollars from my brother to keep me from getting my legs broken, I date this girl, it turns out she used to be a prostitute. So OK, nobody's perfect. Then it turns out she's *still* a prostitute, only now she only does it "on the side," whatever the hell *that* means. I break up with her, I'm scared I'm gonna get AIDS, I can't meet anybody—

**WILLIAM**   Yeah, I get the idea.

**JEFF**   And *then,* William, *then,* I come to you, William, and with your beautiful generosity, you give me this job, you take a little interest in me, and look at me now: I'm payin' my own rent to Marty, buyin' my own groceries. I'm lookin' around for my own place, which'll be the first time I had my own home in six years. My own little living room where I can sit and watch TV; a nice little kitchen I can cook my own meals in . . . Invite a girl over for dinner and be the *only one there with her.* And I'm a healthy happy member of the workforce for nine months straight come Friday. And I'll tell you something else, man, my spirit is OK. I don't have a broken spirit. I just want to stick it out here for at least a year, so I can really get that under my belt—just for my own—just psychologically.

**WILLIAM**   No, I think that's smart—

**JEFF**   Yeah, that's what I told myself. At least one year, right? Day shift, night shift, I don't care. And William, I owe it all to you. So see? You really helped somebody. Now that might just be your good character, but it's my good luck.

**WILLIAM**   Glad to be of service, Jeff. You're doin' all right.

**JEFF**   Thanks, man. I gotta tell you, I feel pretty good.

**WILLIAM**   All right, man. I should get going on my rounds.

*William doesn't move.*

**JEFF**   Hey, have you seen that little cop—what's that big-shot cop's name?

**WILLIAM**   Who, Bill?

**JEFF**   Yeah, Bill. Have you seen his new partner?

15

**WILLIAM**  Yes.

**JEFF**  Can I share something with you? Sometimes I have this fantasy I'm being tied up and interrogated by all these lady cops—Like they have me handcuffed to a chair, and I'm naked, and they're walking around in nothing but their hats and gun belts . . .

**WILLIAM**  (*Not interested*)  You know what, Jeff?

**JEFF**  . . . and the way they get me to talk is by taking turns— you know, doing stuff to me—like, sexually arousing me, see, but only up to a certain point, till I can't take it anymore and I have to tell 'em what they want to know, so I can get some relief.

*Pause.*

**WILLIAM**  What in the world makes you think I'd be interested in that, man?

**JEFF**  I don't know. You think that little cop would be interested? Maybe she'd find it titillating. You know: sexy.

**WILLIAM**  I have no idea. But if I were you I'd just forget about the whole thing because she'll just end up making you feel small.

**JEFF**  Why would you say that?

**WILLIAM**  Because whatever you do, you're just an imitation cop and she's a real cop. And if you get involved with some lady policewoman it is a sure bet you're gonna end up feeling outranked and outclassed.

**JEFF**  I always feel that way. My last girlfriend was a tollbooth collector, and *she* intimidated the shit out of me. At least if I was going out with a cop, I'd feel, you know, somewhat safe.

**WILLIAM**  Go ahead and laugh, man. You know what's gonna happen to you?

**JEFF**  Yeah, I know, the Joker's gonna get me.

*Silence.*

**JEFF**  What's the matter, man? You worried about your brother?

**WILLIAM**  Yeah, I'm pretty worried.

**JEFF**  So but, what did he do?

*William does not respond.*

**JEFF**  What's the matter? You can tell me.

**WILLIAM**  It's not a question of that, Jeff . . .

**JEFF**  I'm not gonna say anything . . . Maybe I could be helpful. Maybe I could give you some special insight into the workings of the fuck-up mind.

**WILLIAM**  I'm sure you could.

**JEFF**  That's OK. I don't wanna . . . I just want to offer my services as a friendly person, that's all. But if it's too private, I understand. No pressure. I don't take it—you know . . . I don't take it personally or anything.

**WILLIAM**  All right . . . I should get going.

**JEFF**  Hey, maybe you should run upstairs and see Mrs. Heinvald for a few minutes before you take off. She's looking unbelievable lately.

**WILLIAM**  No thanks, Jeff.

**JEFF**  Come on, man, I think a little visit to ol' Mrs. Heinvald might be just what you need.

**WILLIAM**   I don't think my wife would appreciate that too much, man.

**JEFF**   All right. I hope your brother's all right.

**WILLIAM**   Thank you. (*Pause*) I'll see you tomorrow.

**JEFF**   I'll be here.

**WILLIAM**   I know you will, Jeff.

*William walks out. Jeff is left alone in the lobby. He locks the door, goes to his station, picks up his paperback novel and starts reading. He gets bored, looks up, and stares off into the long night ahead.*

# ACT ONE, SCENE TWO

*Late the next night. Jeff is in the lobby. Two uniformed police officers,*
BILL, *around thirty, and* DAWN, *early twenties, are on the street*
*outside. Jeff cannot hear them.*

**BILL**  Take it easy, will you? Just take it easy.

**DAWN**  I'm sorry. I guess I'm still a little bit shook up, you
know?

**BILL**  Hey, that is totally natural. I'd be worried if you *weren't*
a little shook up. OK?

**DAWN**  Yeah, OK.

**BILL**  But. Just want you to know, you handled yourself
pretty good back there.

**DAWN**  Yeah? (*Pause*) It was no big deal.

**BILL**  You kept your head, you took control of the situation,
you did exactly what you were supposed to do. OK? You
were great!

**DAWN** (*Delighted*)  Shut up.

**BILL**  I'm serious.

**DAWN**  So but, is there really gonna be like an inquiry?

**BILL**  Yeah, but don't worry about that . . .

**DAWN**  But what do they usually do? Do they—

**BILL**  They just—You gotta go down to the Trial Room . . .
they ask you what happened . . . they ask me what
happened . . . They read your *report*, they read *my* report . . .
Then they say OK, thanks, and that's it. Don't worry about

it. Anyway, that guy's gonna be fine . . . I mean, I personally wouldn'ta hit him quite that *hard* . . . But that's a judgment call. You know? Plus the fact is, if *I* hit him like that he'd probably be dead right now.

**DAWN**  Yeah, well, for a minute there I thought he *was* dead, you know?

**BILL**  Believe me. That guy is fine. Don't worry about it. Besides, he totally had it comin'.

**DAWN**  You told me you gotta establish yourself . . .

**BILL**  Absolutely. No question about it. I don't think there's an officer in the Division, male or female, wouldn'ta done the exact same thing the exact same way. Only probably not as good.

**DAWN**  Thanks. (*Pause*) That means a lot, comin' from you.

**BILL**  What do you mean?

**DAWN**  (*Looking at her shoes*)  Well you know—I mean— that's all.

**BILL**  What did I ever do to deserve such high praise?

**DAWN**  You? Oh, only nothin'.

**BILL**  Seriously.

**DAWN**  What did you *do*—? Come on.

*She shakes her head, smiling.*

**BILL**  You like the way I handle myself.

**DAWN**  Uh, slightly. Yeah.

**BILL**  But what do you *think* of me? Seriously now. What do you think of *me*?

**DAWN**  I think you're—I think you're the most dedicated person I ever met.

**BILL**  Don't butter me up.

**DAWN**  I think you're the best cop I ever saw.

**BILL**  No shit?

**DAWN**  Don't ask me questions if you don't want a straight answer. I don't fuck around. You want to know something all you gotta do is ask me. You want a lot of bullshit you can go talk to Lieutenant Finelli or whatever his fuckin' name is.

**BILL**  You don't like Bob Finelli?

**DAWN**  I don't care. He can talk shit if he wants. I don't care.

**BILL**  So I'm the best cop you ever saw?

**DAWN**  You heard what I said. You also got a swelled head the size of . . . somethin' really big, but you're the kind of cop I'd like to be, and that's the truth.

**BILL**  You're fulla crap.

**DAWN**  No—

**BILL**  All those guys've been filling your head with a lotta shit. So don't pay too much attention to any kind of flashy stories you mighta heard about me. You know last month? When I got my commendation—now that's the fifth year in a row I got that commendation. So *what*? I'm finally on the list to get my gold shield, these guys are runnin' around Jerry McAllen's house, sayin' shit about me, callin' me Supercop, and I—Frank Hall. Gives me this T-shirt with a—with one of them photographs, you can get the photograph put on the T-shirt. . . ?

**DAWN** (*Smiling*)  Yeah . . . ?

**BILL**  And he had this T-shirt made with my head on a picture of Superman—underneath it says "Super Bill." But that is *bull*shit.

**DAWN**  I don't think it's bullshit.

**BILL**  OK, tough guy.

*She is smiling openly, embarrassed.*

**BILL**  What are you smilin' like that for?

**DAWN** (*Turning away*)  I don't know.

**BILL**  What are you turnin' away for?

**DAWN**  I'm not turning away.

**BILL**  What are you, flirting with me?

**DAWN**  No.

**BILL**  You flirting with your partner?

**DAWN**  No . . . !

**BILL**  That's against the law, you know.

**DAWN**  No it's not. I'm not doin' it, but it's not against the law if I was.

**BILL**  Any more of this and I'm gonna sue your ass for sexual harassment.

**DAWN**  Yeah, right, I think it's a little late for that.

*Pause. They look at each other.*

**BILL**  All right. I'm gonna go up and see my friend Jim for a few minutes, and then we're gonna get back to work. Then after we sign out, we'll go get ourselves a little drink . . . ? If you want. If not, I totally understand.

*Long pause.*

**DAWN**  All right.

**BILL**  All right, good. (*Pause*) Now straighten up and try to behave yourself—good-looking.

**DAWN**  I'll try.

*They go into the lobby. Jeff looks up from his book.*

**JEFF**  Evening, guys.

**BILL**  I'm just going to 22–J. You don't have to call up.

*Bill moves past him toward the exit to the elevators.*

**JEFF**  Sorry—Officer? Officer? Could I just get your autograph here?

*He gestures to his visitor sign-in book. Bill misunderstands him.*

**BILL**  (*Pleased*)  You want my autograph?

**JEFF**  If you don't mind.

**BILL**  All right . . .

*Bill approaches the desk and breaks out his pen.*

**BILL**  So how do you know who I am?

**JEFF**  I don't know. I've seen you *around* . . . Who are you?

**BILL**  You just told me you wanted an autograph.

**JEFF**  Oh—No, I just meant could you sign in, in my book here. I was just using an amusing form of words.

*Bill looks at him and puts his pen away. Dawn is amused.*

**BILL** (*To Dawn*)  I'll be down in a few minutes.

**JEFF**  Actually—Officer? I'm sorry. If you could just sign in, that'd be—

**BILL**  Don't worry about it, it's all right.

*Bill exits. Jeff signs him in. Dawn waits. Jeff looks at her. Long pause.*

**JEFF**  How you doin'?

**DAWN**  Good.

**JEFF**  Busy night?

**DAWN**  Not so busy.

**JEFF**  Things have really been hoppin' around here, I gotta tell you.

**DAWN**  Oh yeah?

**JEFF**  Oh my God, I haven't had a minute to sit down. People comin' *in* the lobby, people goin' *out* of the lobby. Elevator goin' up, elevator goin' down. *Thoughts* flyin' in and out of my head: It's been crazy.

**DAWN**  Maybe you better just slow it down.

**JEFF** (*Gesturing to the busy lobby around him*)  How can I?

**DAWN**  I don't know.

**JEFF**  Hey, can I ask you something, Officer?

**DAWN**  Yeah?

**JEFF**  Do you know why the New York City cops changed from the light blue shirts to the dark blue shirts recently? Like a couple of years ago?

**DAWN**  No, why?

**JEFF**  No—I'm not sayin' like, "Do you know," and then like I tell you the *answer*. I'm really asking, 'cause I thought you might know.

**DAWN**  Oh. No. I don't.

**JEFF**  But remember how a long time ago, like when we were kids, the police uniforms used to be all dark blue? And then around the 1980s I guess, they switched to the dark blue pants and a light blue shirt? And then recently they switched 'em back to the dark blue pants and a dark blue shirt again? What *I* always wondered was, did they throw out all the old dark blue pants when they did that? Or did they just throw out the light blue shirts and then get dark blue shirts that matched the old dark blue pants, so they wouldn't have to buy all new pants? Because that would be quite a savings.

**DAWN**  I have no idea.

**JEFF**  If you think about it, you could be wearing pants right now that were being worn by some lady cop in 1975, if you think about it. Except I guess the women police officers didn't wear pants back in 1975. I don't mean they didn't wear *pants*, like they were walkin' around in their underwear. I just mean I think they were still wearin' skirts back then, weren't they? I know I'm blathering, I'm just completely in love with you—can I just say that?

**DAWN**  OK, take it easy.

**JEFF**  No, I am, man: I seen you go by a lot over the last few weeks and I just think you are *it,* man; I'd do anything if you would just give me the time of *day.*

**DAWN**  OK—

**JEFF** And it's not just because I'm intrigued by the feminine mystique of the female cop—

**DAWN** All right—

**JEFF** And I don't mean any disrespect—

**DAWN** Oh of course not.

**JEFF** Your generation of lady cops are like *pioneers* as far as I'm concerned. I think you guys are *great*. But I also happen to find most of you extremely sexy, OK?

**DAWN** Get outta here.

**JEFF** How long have you been a cop?

**DAWN** I don't know. How long you been a doorman?

*Pause.*

**JEFF** No, I'm not a doorman. I'm a security officer.

**DAWN** Congratulations. Now how about givin' me a break.

**JEFF** Sure. Fine. (*Pause*) Givin' the cop a break. (*Pause*) I guess it's just the gun, and the handcuffs . . . the big stick.

**DAWN** All right already!

**JEFF** Hey, look: You're wearin' a uniform and I'm wearin' a uniform.

**DAWN** So?

**JEFF** So we both got uniforms. Let's get together.

**DAWN** You meet a lot of girls this way?

**JEFF** No, hardly any. (*Pause*) What do you work, ten to six?

**DAWN** So?

**JEFF**   Just askin'. I'm on twelve to eight. But I don't mind it. It's quiet. Plus, like, that's the other thing: Not a lot of people come in after one or two A.M., so I always have a newspaper, see, so what I do is after two I lock the door, and I take the newspaper, and I sit like this . . . (*Putting the newspaper in front of his face*) . . . so it looks like I'm reading the paper, and I can just sleep that way. And if somebody's at the door they knock, and if somebody comes downstairs the elevator dings, and I just swing around and here I am. (*He demonstrates.*) See?

**DAWN**   Oh yeah, if I lived here that'd make me feel real safe.

**JEFF**   They feel safe. They don't know I'm sleeping. But I actually—See, this is just temporary for me. I've only been doin' this nine months. And it's a good job, but I couldn't be a security guard my whole life. You know? I'm way too restless. Plus I lived all over the world when I was a kid, 'cause my Dad was in the Navy, and then I was in the Navy, so I know there's a bigger world out there. I really actually want to get into advertising, is what my dream is.

**DAWN**   Oh yeah . . . ?

**JEFF**   I don't mean that to sound too pathetic, like "How's *this* guy ever gonna get into advertising?" But I often thought that that could be a field that I might be kind of good at. Thinkin' up funny slogans for things . . .

**DAWN**   Uh-huh . . . ?

**JEFF**   . . . Thinkin' up different ways to advertise things. Well, I know it's probably a pretty hard field to get into, obviously, so at this point it's pretty much in fantasy land, but . . . (*Pause*) Must be interesting being a cop.

**DAWN**   It's interesting.

**JEFF**  You're a rookie, right? Come on, I can tell you're a rookie.

**DAWN**  Oh yeah?

**JEFF**  Boy, you must have a lot of guts. That's all I can say. I mean I know it takes guts just to be a cop in the first place, but to be a woman cop? That takes guts. Hats off to you. I'm not kidding.

**DAWN**  Yeah, well, I wouldn't know about that.

**JEFF**  Are there a lot of cops in your family or something?

**DAWN**  I'm the first.

**JEFF**  Good for you, man. That's awesome. I'm the first security guard in my family.

**DAWN**  Oh yeah?

**JEFF**  Yeah. It's kind of a point of pride with me.

**DAWN**  Yeah, I could see that.

**JEFF**  Hey, is it true that a female cop—(*As she starts to bristle*) Now wait a minute, this is not bullshit; I'm really curious.

**DAWN**  Yeah . . . ?

**JEFF**  Is it true that a female cop is likelier to shoot her gun or use her weapon or whatever than a male cop because she can't—you know, because she can't overpower you in any other way?

**DAWN**  No. That's a myth. They teach you a lot more than shooting, believe me.

**JEFF**  Really? Like what? (*Stepping back*) I'm not asking for a demonstration, I'm just asking like what do they teach you. Have you been involved in—

28

**DAWN**  (on "been") they teach you a lot of things; you just try to control the situation.

| JEFF | DAWN |
|------|------|
| So like how do you— | Like tonight we had to break up this brawl— |

**JEFF**  Oh yeah? I'm sorry—

**DAWN**  That is all right. So we get there and these two guys are goin' at it outside this restaurant, right? So Bill—that's my partner—

**JEFF** (*Overlapping*)  Uh-huh? Yeah, I know—

**DAWN**  —he pulls this one guy away, and I go, "OK, let's break it up." So then this big fat guy whips around, he says, "Why? What are *you* gonna do about it, bitch?" Then he starts *chargin'* me.

**JEFF**  Really? This is a fantastic story!

**DAWN**  Oh yeah. But what you do is you just pivot back, like you pivot back and then you bring your nightstick up—you know, not to take their head off, but just to bring 'em down. Except I guess I got a little enthusiastic and I really whacked this guy, and that was it. Boom.

**JEFF**  What do you mean, boom? What happened to him?

**DAWN**  Nothin'. He had to go to the hospital.

**JEFF**  Really? You put him in the hospital?

**DAWN**  Oh yeah. You shoulda seen him. There was fuckin' blood *every*where. It was superficial of course. But your head can really bleed a lot.

**JEFF**  So . . . don't take this the wrong way, but would that qualify as police brutality at all?

**DAWN**  No. No way! He was totally comin' at me. And this guy was huge. But then, naturally of course two seconds later his wife comes outta the restaurant and she's screamin' "I'm an attorney, I'm callin' the CCRB, I'm gonna sue you . . ."

**JEFF**  Calling the who?

**DAWN**
The CCRB? The Civilian
Complaint Review Board?
Which—you know—is
definitely their right

**JEFF**
Oh, yeah, OK, yeah.

to do that. But that could be kinda serious for me, 'cause I'm still on my Probation? Like your first six months you're not like a full cop. You're what they call a Probationary Officer. And if you can't handle it or you just screw up, you're just out. You're off the Force. But Bill saw the whole thing and he says it's no problem. So I gotta go through a little song and dance. Big deal.

**JEFF**  And you didn't have to use your gun.

**DAWN**  Oh no. Definitely not. He was just some stupid drunk.

**JEFF**  But are you a pretty good shot?

**DAWN**  Yeah. I'm OK.

**JEFF**  That's excellent. (*Pause*) So what's he doin' up there anyway? Investigatin' a crime or somethin'?

**DAWN**  No, he's just saying hello to a friend.

**JEFF**  He's a friend of Mrs. Heinvald?

*Pause.*

**DAWN**  Who?

**JEFF**  Mrs. Heinvald. The lady in 22–J.

**DAWN** (*Confused*)  No. Yeah. (*Pause*) 22–J—Yeah. I guess so. (*Pause*) *I* don't know her. *I* don't know who lives there.

**JEFF**  Well, I don't wanna say nothin', but he's liable to be up there a long time.

**DAWN**  What's it to you?

**JEFF**  I didn't say anything. I just don't see why you should have to cool your heels in the lobby eating your heart out while he's upstairs gettin' laid.

*Pause.*

**DAWN**  He's not gettin' laid.

**JEFF**  Oh, come on.

**DAWN**  Hey, look: First of all—we're in the middle of our shift.

**JEFF**  Oh my God, excuse me, you're right, it's impossible.

*Pause.*

**DAWN**  Who did you say lives in that apartment?

**JEFF**  Mrs. Heinvald. Amy Heinvald. She's an actress or a model or something. She's divorced. She's . . .

**DAWN**  Have you seen him here a lot?

**JEFF**  Sure, I seen him a few times. How long you been working together?

*Pause.*

**DAWN**  What makes you think he's . . . you know.

**JEFF**  Because the lady he's visiting has a very active social schedule, if you see what I mean.

**DAWN**  No. I don't.

**JEFF**  I just mean she—

**DAWN**  What do you mean?

**JEFF**  I mean she's got a lot of boyfriends. That's all.

*Dawn's heart slowly breaks.*

**JEFF**  Hey, don't listen to me. I don't know what I'm talking about. Maybe I'm wrong. Maybe your partner is like, her favorite uncle or something.

**DAWN**  Yeah.

*She moves away from him.*

**JEFF**  Hey . . . how come male cops are so big and fat and female cops are so young and beautiful?

**DAWN**  Yeah, how come doormen never know when to shut up?

**JEFF**  I don't know. That's an interesting point. Only I wouldn't be able to comment on it because I'm not a doorman. I'm a security guard.

**DAWN**  I don't fucking believe this.

**JEFF**  Hey, the guy is only human. You gotta *see* this lady—

**DAWN**  Hey, look: I'm not talking about him. I don't even— Look, you wanna know something? I don't even know why I'm *talking* to you. And if my partner wants to take time off his shift to go get laid with Mrs. Whatever-She-Is, you know what? More power to him, that's what I say—

**JEFF**  I agree!

**DAWN**  Because I seen him do more good for more people than anybody I ever met in my *life*. And if he wants to see that *model* in 22–J, that is his business, not mine—

**JEFF**  Sure!

**DAWN**  —and not yours. And I don't need to get *hit* on by the night *doorman* while he's upstairs gettin' his rocks off with some fuckin' whore.

| JEFF | DAWN |
|---|---|
| Hey lady, I am not a door-man, I'm a security guard. I told you three fuckin' times already— In fact, I'm a security *specialist*! So— | I don't give a shit what you are, just keep your mouth shut! Good! Just keep your mouth shut! You talk to me, you keep your mouth shut, you understand? |

**JEFF**  What?

**DAWN**  What?

*Pause.*

| JEFF | DAWN |
|---|---|
| How can I talk to you and keep my mouth shut at the same time? | Forget it. For*get* about it. For*get* about it. |

*Pause.*

**JEFF**  I'm not trying to make trouble.

**DAWN**  Just stop trying to pick me up.

33

**JEFF**   I'm not trying to pick you up—

**DAWN**   Why don't you try speaking to me like I was an officer of the law? Just like, as an experiment.

**JEFF**   I'm sorry. I'm not usually this attracted to police officers.

**DAWN**   Well, you're lucky.

*She moves away from him. Pause.*

**JEFF**   What's your name?

**DAWN**   Officer Wilson.

**JEFF**   Oh come on. What's your name? (*Pause*) Are you a sports fan? Come on. That's a harmless question. What do you like, basketball? A lot of girls like basketball. It's graceful. Well, a lot of sports are very graceful though, actually. What's your feeling about the impending garbage strike? My name's Jeff. Twenty-seven, never been married, never been in debt. Well, I have been in a little bit of debt actually, but that's pretty much all cleared up now. I'm a different person now. Really. I've turned over a whole new leaf—

**DAWN**   Would you shut *up*?

**JEFF**   Sure, I'd be glad to. Why don't *you* say something for a few seconds and then I'll say something back and we'll go on like that. I'm a Goddamn security guard for Christ's sake. I'm lonely as shit. There's three other guys in this building and I never see them except on the video screen. I'll shut up. I'd love to hear somebody else talk.

**DAWN**   I just don't feel like it right this minute.

**JEFF**   I understand. I'm not trying to make trouble. And don't listen to me. I don't know what he's doin' up there. I don't know anything about it.

**DAWN**  Hey, what do I care? The fucking guy is married anyway.

*Jeff goes back to his station and picks up his book. Long silence.*

**DAWN**  Can you believe this shit?

**JEFF**  (*Puts down his book*)  Yeah . . . They probably don't warn you about this kind of thing in the Police Academy.

**DAWN**  (*A bitter joke*)  Sure they do. I took a seminar.

**JEFF**  What happens if there's a major outbreak of crime on your beat under these circumstances?

**DAWN**  Oh, then I'm supposed to buzz him.

**JEFF**  Are there are lot of romances between cops?

**DAWN**  I don't know . . . Some of them get married.

**JEFF**  No, but, I mean like illicit, kind of behind-the-scenes in the back of the squad car type romances.

**DAWN**  *You're* gonna end up in the back of the squad car in a minute.

**JEFF**  But seriously, is that a pretty widespread problem?

**DAWN**  I'm sure it's no different than other kinds of jobs.

**JEFF**  Well, in other kinds of jobs people have affairs all the time.

**DAWN**  Well.

*Pause.*

**JEFF**  Are you in love with that guy?

**DAWN**  Who.

**JEFF**  You know. Your partner. (*Pause*) Because if you are, I would say that you were in love with the wrong guy.

**DAWN**  I'm not in love with anybody. I just admired him, that's all. OK? He made life a little easier for me in the Department. OK? I mean, you look up to somebody, you take them seriously—and then—That's all. OK?

**JEFF**  OK. (*Pause*) I think it's great what you're doing. (*Pause*) Your family must be proud of you.

**DAWN**  Oh, they think I'm nuts. (*Pause*) Well, not exactly, I mean, my mother thinks I'm a little bit nuts, but I happen to think that she's nuts too, so there's no harm done there, right?

**JEFF**  You have a lot of brothers? I bet you have a lot of—

**DAWN**  (*On "bet"*)  But I guess generally they're proud . . . I was near the top of my class at the Academy . . . I just . . . I just fucked up with *this* prick, that's all. And now I'm *screwed*. Because I obviously really misjudged him, you know? And for all I know he's been shootin' his mouth off all over the department. And it wouldn't have been so hard to avoid the whole thing in the first place. But these guys . . . I mean, they seen so much horrible shit, it's like they don't give a damn about anything. So you gotta walk around like you don't give a damn about anything either. But they know you still do. And they wanna like, stamp it out of you or something. And like, test you, all the time. And it's always like: "Hey—you're not men, you're not women: You're cops. Act like cops and you'll be treated like cops." Only then it turns out they got a pool going as to who's gonna fuck you first, OK? And that's fine. I can handle it. You *make* them respect you. But then somebody decent comes along, and goes out of his way to make life

36

easier for you—and I didn't even *ask* him, because I didn't expect anything different—I didn't *want* anything different. And then, Oh my God, it's true love—Except when he comes down in that elevator, just watch: because *I'm* gonna be the one who's gonna be supposed to act like I'm a cop! I mean . . . (*Pause*) And then I got *you.*

**JEFF**  So far I'm like the nicest guy in the whole story.

**DAWN**  Yeah . . . !

**JEFF**  So why don't you tell me your name?

**DAWN**  Because maybe I don't feel like it, Jeff.

**JEFF**  OK. You don't have to tell me your name. But, uh, do you want to, uh, do you want to go to a basketball game with me tomorrow afternoon? I got tickets to the Knicks game.

**DAWN**  I don't like basketball.

**JEFF**  OK. Well, um, after I'm finished watchin' the basketball game with my *mother,* would you like to go dancing with me? I don't want to get you on the rebound or anything, but I don't know if I'm ever gonna see you again . . . I know I'll see your *partner* again . . . Sorry. I'm sorry.

**DAWN**  I don't care.

**JEFF**  . . . We'll put on our dress uniforms, we'll go dancin', get bombed and come to work.

*Dawn starts crying and turns away.*

**DAWN**  God damn it . . . !

**JEFF**  What's the matter?

**DAWN**  I can't be cryin' on duty . . . !

**JEFF**  Come on . . . You'll drive around, you'll shoot some perpetrators, you'll feel better.

**DAWN**  He is a son of a bitch . . . !

**JEFF**  You know what? You're damn right. And I'll tell you something else—

*Offstage the elevator pings. They both look sharp as Bill enters. (NOTE: He is hatless now.)*

**BILL**  OK. You ready?

**DAWN**  Yeah.

**BILL**  What's the matter?

**DAWN**  Nothin'. What do you mean?

**BILL**  You got a funny look on your face.

**DAWN** (*Shrugs*)  I don't know how I look.

*Dawn looks away. Bill looks at Jeff.*

**BILL** (*To Jeff*)  How you doin'?

**JEFF**  I'm fine. How are you?

**BILL**  I'm fine too. (*To Dawn*) OK?

**DAWN**  Yeah. Let's go.

**BILL** (*To Jeff*)  Hey, if you see William around, tell him Bill says hello.

**JEFF**  Sure thing.

*They go outside and exit. Jeff picks up his book, but he can't concentrate and throws it down. He does nothing for a while.*

*William enters onto the street and comes into the lobby.*

**JEFF**  Hey, William. How you doin'?

**WILLIAM**  Hello Jeff. How's it going?

**JEFF**  Pretty good. The police were just here, but they didn't ask about you, and I signed them right in. It was that cop Bill and his partner. He said tell William Bill says hi.

**WILLIAM**  Was that all?

**JEFF**  That was all.

**WILLIAM**  (*Sitting down*)  OK . . .

**JEFF**  Oh, yeah, and I told Manuel to clean up the desk.

**WILLIAM**  (*Takes out cigarettes*)  What?

**JEFF**  I said, I told Manuel to clean up the desk—to straighten up the desk drawers—

**WILLIAM**  Oh yeah, yeah, thank you.

**JEFF**  I really laid into him, too, because this desk is disgusting. I mean, when you open this drawer it should be *spotless*. I told him I want to be able to eat my *breakfast* outta this drawer tomorrow morning. I told him you were ready to kill somebody about these drawers. I really did.

**WILLIAM**  OK, Jeff. Thanks.

**JEFF**  You're welcome. Taken care of. (*Long pause*) You're not very chatty tonight . . .

**WILLIAM**  What?

**JEFF**  I said you're not very chatty tonight. You're not really holding up your end of the conversation very well.

**WILLIAM**  Sorry, Jeff, I've got a lot on my mind.

**JEFF**  That's OK. We don't have to talk about anything. I'm just glad to see your smiling face.

**WILLIAM**  Same here, Jeff. You just keep talking. If I hear anything worth responding to I'll just jump in.

**JEFF**  OK. (*Pause*) How's your brother doing?

**WILLIAM**  I don't know. I haven't spoken to him.

**JEFF**  Did you find out what he did? Oh no, you knew what he did, you just didn't want to tell *me* about it. That's OK. I forgot. That's completely fine. I don't mean to sound so inquisitive. I'm sorry. (*Pause*) So did you see where the Mayor says he's gonna shut down all the—

**WILLIAM** (*On "shut"*)  All right, let me ask you something, Jeff. Suppose somebody who's supposed to be near and dear to you was accused of doing some kind of terrible crime, and was trying to use you as an alibi. What would you do, for example, if it was a false alibi? That is to say, you weren't with the person when they said that you were?

**JEFF**  I don't know. I guess it would depend on who they were and what . . .

**WILLIAM**  Yeah, see, we already part company. I like to tell the truth.

**JEFF**  Well, so do I—

**WILLIAM**  What are you talking about, man? I didn't even get through the details of the hypothetical situation and you're already gearing up to perjure yourself.

**JEFF**  No I'm not. I was just—I mean if it was my *mother* or something—

**WILLIAM**  Right, because that's what everybody expects, right?

But that's where I part company with ninety-five percent of the human race. So I'm a freak. But I wouldn't do it.

**JEFF**  Are you talking—I assume you're talking about your brother?

**WILLIAM**  It doesn't matter who I'm talking about.

**JEFF**  So but what did he do?

**WILLIAM**  I don't know what he did, man, because he hasn't been tried in a court of law.

**JEFF**  What are you, some kind of Robotron? What did they *accuse* him of?

*Pause.*

**WILLIAM**  They say—They arrested him and two friends for allegedly going into a hospital last night to steal pharmaceutical drugs, and some nurse apparently saw them and they attacked her—

**JEFF**  Oh my God . . .

**WILLIAM**  . . . and they beat her up with a pipe or something like that, and now she's dead.

**JEFF**  Oh my *God* . . .

**WILLIAM**  . . . And according to my brother's girlfriend, my brother told the police I was with him at the time at some movie.

**JEFF**  Wow.

**WILLIAM**  Yeah, gave her a whole made-up schedule what we were supposedly doing last night for me to memorize: What movie, who called who, what time we ate, who ate what, you wouldn't believe it. See, he can't handle getting a job or applying himself to go to school, but he has the wherewithal to come up with *that* shit on the spur of the moment when he's in the jailhouse under arrest for murder at two o'clock in the morning.

**JEFF**  Wow.

**WILLIAM**  "Wow."

**JEFF**  Well, would—I mean, God, I mean—do you—

**WILLIAM**  And it's not like . . . See, his girlfriend called me tonight, and apparently two of my brother's friends—these *real* criminals, mind—were identified by some doctor, and the cops picked them up and they named my brother as the third guy. But the doctor didn't really get a good look at him, so they're trying to dig up something substantial that would link him to the scene, and meanwhile my brother says he was at home alone, no alibi, and so would I say he was at the movies with me last night?

**JEFF**  Jesus Christ.

**WILLIAM**  See, I don't think *he'd* ever do anything that fuckin' heinous, but he's definitely done a lot of other shit. And I know these guys he's always with, and . . . You know, I want to be objective about it, to some degree. I want to . . . I can't just be saying, "Well, seeing how he's my brother, it is therefore impossible for him to have done this ghastly thing." You know what I mean?

**JEFF**  Yeah . . .

**WILLIAM**  I just wish I had more information. But who am I gonna talk to? His girlfriend? She just parrots everything he says; she's got no will of her own. And what's *he* gonna tell me? That he's guilty? He knows what I'll do then.

**JEFF**  Yeah . . . Wow.

**WILLIAM**   And I am not the type of person who sympathizes with the criminal element in this kind of situation. Not at all. But the fact remains that there's a lot of people in jail who don't belong there, a lot of black people in jail who don't belong there, and a lot of cops and prosecutors and what have you who would just as soon throw somebody in jail as nobody. And I hate to say it, but my brother is tailor-made for the part; and if he's being railroaded in some way, I don't know what right I may have to my private reservations. So it's an interesting dilemma. It's interesting. But I'll tell you something, Jeff, and you can quote me on this right now: If he had anything to do with killing that woman I'd sooner put a bullet through his head myself than lift a finger to help him. Because that is inhuman. Inhuman. Even if he was just standing *by* . . . Some innocent person . . . And all she did was show up at work that night? (*Pause*) But we're hoping it's all some terrible misunderstanding, right?

**JEFF**   Right. Right.

**WILLIAM**   So what would *you* do there, Jeff?

**JEFF**   Me? Oh, well, the first thing I would do is I would definitely try to find out if my brother was with those guys or not. Because that could really inform the whole situation right there.

*Pause.*

**WILLIAM**   Well no fuckin' shit, Jeff. How in the world do you expect me to do that?

**JEFF**
Don't get mad at me, you asked me what I would do!

**WILLIAM**
Well what the fuck do you expect me to do? "Find out if he was there or not."

43

All right, all right!                Hot *dog,* I never
                                     would have thought of *that.*
All right!

**WILLIAM**  If I could just find *that* out the rest of this shit
might just fall right into place!

**JEFF**
Well can't you go see him?       **WILLIAM**
Can't you talk to him?           No I can't go see him,
You'll be able to tell           Goddamn it, he's locked
whether or not he's              up in fuckin' Rikers
lying—                           Island! I can't go see
                                 him till after the arraignment!

OK, what about his girl-
friend? Maybe you should         I already talked to her,
go see her—                      Jeff! Look, look, I don't
                                 actually expect you to solve
                                 this for me. Let's just forget I
                                 brought it up.

**JEFF**  I'm sorry. This kind of problem is not exactly within
my forte.

**WILLIAM**  Which is what?

*Pause.*

**JEFF**
OK, you don't have to            **WILLIAM**
get nasty, I'm only              What is your forte, man?
tryin' to be—                    What is your forte?

*Pause.*

**JEFF**  I don't have one. Losing money.

**WILLIAM**  All right, never mind, Jeff. Thanks anyway.

44

*Pause.*

**JEFF**  Do you know if the nurse was white or black?

**WILLIAM**  No.

| | |
|---|---|
| **JEFF** | **WILLIAM** |
| Because that could— | What difference does that make? |

**JEFF**  It's just if she's white there's probably gonna be a big stink about it in the papers, and if she's black they probably won't play it up as much.

**WILLIAM**  Well, I don't know what color she was . . . I just better figure out what I'm gonna do before the cops catch up with me, because I'm not gonna get two chances to do this right.

*William gets up.*

**JEFF**  Is there anything you want me to tell the cops if they show up?

**WILLIAM**  (*Stops*)  What?

**JEFF**  If the cops come by and ask me if I've seen you?

**WILLIAM**  Tell them you saw me.

**JEFF**  What if they ask me if you talked about your brother? What should I tell 'em?

**WILLIAM**  Maybe it'd be better if you didn't mention any of that till I figure out what I'm doing.

**JEFF**  (*A joke*)  Well—I don't feel comfortable *lying* to them.

**WILLIAM**  OK. Well . . . In that case, just—

**JEFF**  No I was just—I'm just kidding.

**WILLIAM**  Oh.

**JEFF**  Sorry.

*Pause.*

**WILLIAM**  What the fuck do you find funny about this, man?

**JEFF**  Nothing. I'm really sorry. I really apologize.

**WILLIAM**  All right. I should get going.

*They see Bill and Dawn enter onto the street. Bill says a word to Dawn and comes into the lobby. Dawn stays outside.*

**WILLIAM**  Hey there, Bill.

**BILL**  (*Shaking hands*)  Hey William. How you doin'?

**WILLIAM**  Oh, I'm all right. Do you know Jeff? Jeff, Bill.

**JEFF**  Yeah, we met before.

**BILL**  So how you doin' these days, William? All right?

**WILLIAM**  I'm pretty well. Can't complain.

**BILL**  Yeah? Things goin' all right?

**WILLIAM**  More or less, yeah.

**BILL**  Good . . . Good . . . That's good. So listen . . . Could I talk to you for a minute?

**WILLIAM**  Sure.

*Bill takes William aside.*

**BILL**  So listen . . . I heard about the whole thing with your brother, and I was in the neighborhood, and I just thought I'd come down and just talk to you a little bit in case I could be helpful. But I don't want you to feel nervous; this is totally unofficial, OK? You know what? Don't even say OK. Just listen to me: Now I understand he's possibly putting you in a very bad position—(*William starts to speak.*) Please! Don't say anything. Just listen for a second. I just want to say that I don't know if you were really with him the other night or not, and I don't want to know. It's not my case, it's not my problem. Now, I'm sure you heard what happened to that nurse, so I'm not gonna go into that, but we're talking about a twenty-seven-year-old single mother, three children. OK? And I just want to say, if you were *not* with him last night, you're gonna need to talk to somebody. And I want you to know I'm available any time of the night or day. OK? I'm not gonna—you know—there's only so much I can do, of course, but I want you to know I'm here, I'm not judgin' you, I wanna try to help you out, and I'm gonna do everything I can for you within the law and maybe a little bit around the edges, OK? Just don't quote me on that. Now, I'm gonna give you my beeper number (*Writing on his card*) and this is my *home* number. OK? And I want you to *use* this. All right?

*He gives the card to William.*

**WILLIAM**  Hey, Bill—

**BILL**  No no, just think about what I said and gimme a call. OK? I'll stop by tomorrow, maybe we could just have a cup of coffee and talk. OK? Don't even say OK. Just say good night.

**WILLIAM**  Good night, Bill.

*They shake hands.*

**BILL**  Now if you don't mind, I just wanna talk to your friend here for a couple of minutes. OK? Just need a little privacy.

**WILLIAM** (*Surprised*) Oh—No—All right. I'll just, uh, I'll just go on about my rounds.

**BILL** OK, buddy. See you later. And *call* me.

**WILLIAM** See you later, Jeff.

**JEFF** Good night, Will.

*William goes onto the street and exits. Bill and Jeff are alone. Dawn is still outside on the street. She can't quite hear what's going on inside but she can get the gist.*

**JEFF** What can I do for you, Officer?

**BILL** Jeff, right?

**JEFF** Yeah.

**BILL** Well, listen to me, Jeff. I don't appreciate people discussing my private business when I'm not around. OK? You got anything to tell my partner about me or my friends or the people I visit in this building or anywhere else, say it in front of my fuckin' face, so I could get a chance to stick up for myself and not spend the rest of my night defending myself against a bunch of bullshit that was dumped on me by some fuckin' idiot when I'm not even around to defend myself. OK?

**JEFF** (*Muttering, intimidated*) Yeah . . .

**BILL** What?

**JEFF** I said yeah! I'm sorry. I didn't . . .

**BILL** What do you think it makes you a big man, tellin' her my business?

**JEFF** No.

**BILL** How do you know what I'm doin' up there?

48

**JEFF**   I don't.

**BILL**   That's not what you told her.

**JEFF**   I don't know what I told her . . .

**BILL**   OK: Let's ask her. Hey DAWN!

**JEFF**   Oh is that her name?

**BILL**   What?

**JEFF**   Nothin'—We don't have to call her in here—

**BILL**   What's the matter? Why not?

*During this exchange, on the street Dawn has turned toward them.*
*Bill gestures for her to stay put. She hesitates, then stays put.*

**JEFF**   —You really—You made your point.

**BILL**   All right. Now you listen to me. Look out there: What
do you see out there?

*Jeff looks out at Dawn.*

**JEFF**   I don't really know what you—

**BILL**   What do you see out there?

*Pause.*

**JEFF**   I'm sorry. I don't understand what you m—

**BILL**   Do you see a police officer? You see a piece of ass? I
mean, what?

*Pause.*

**JEFF**   I see a police officer piece of ass.

**BILL**   What do you think I'm joking with you?

**JEFF**   No.

**BILL**  You think it's some big joke?

**JEFF**  No.

**BILL**  You want me to tell you what *I* see out there?

**JEFF**  Sure.

**BILL**  I see a little girl wearin' a police uniform. OK? I see a little girl from the neighborhood who some moron told her she could be a cop. But she's not a cop right now. But if somebody takes a shot at her, or somebody else's life depends on her, they're not gonna know she's not a cop. They're gonna think she knows what she's doing. She walks around the corner where somebody's trying to rob somebody or rape somebody or kill somebody, they're not gonna know she's a little girl in a cop suit; they're gonna see a badge and a uniform and a gun and they're gonna blow a hole through her fuckin' head. Somebody runs up to her and asks her to help 'em she's not gonna help 'em, she's gonna look around and say, "Where's Bill? Where's Bill?"—That's me: I'm Bill. Now, I could tell that girl likes me. It's only natural. I'm her partner, I'm a big strong father figure, whatever, gotta lot of experience, gotta lotta confidence, I know what I'm fuckin' doin'—and that's attractive to a woman, it's attractive to anybody. So she's attracted to me. That's OK. She's human. I'm human. But maybe part of what I'm doin', part of buildin' her confidence is makin' her feel like I'm interested in her too. Maybe that makes her feel impressive. Makes her feel cocky, makes her feel like she's got something on the ball. Makes her feel like she's really a *cop*. Now, do I need you tellin' her I'm upstairs havin' *sex* with somebody on my *shift* so she can think I'm some kind of fuckin' *maniac* who's just messin' with her head, so she can lose all her confidence in me and consequently all her confidence in herself? Because of your big fuckin' flappin' fuckin' mouth? And then go out and get herself killed? Or me? Or somebody else? This is not a game. We're not *door*men. We're *police*men. Yeah, I know, we're terrible and everything, but we're playing with our *lives,* and the lives of the people we're supposed to protect. So I don't appreciate the fun I guess you're havin' at my expense and more importantly at her expense, while you're sitting around here twiddling your fuckin' thumbs and waiting for, uh, William to come around and make his rounds so you can go to *sleep.* OK?

**JEFF**   Yeah.

**BILL**   You know what I really feel like doin'? I really feel like smacking the shit outta you. But I'm not gonna do that, because I don't do that. Just when I come around here in future, just be aware that you don't know what I'm doing here, you have no idea, and keep your fuckin' nose outta my business. You understand me?

**JEFF**   Yes.

**BILL**   OK. The discussion's over now.

*Bill goes outside. Jeff's buzzer buzzes. He answers it, talks briefly into the phone, then hangs up. During the following, although he can't hear what they are saying, he edges closer to the lobby door and waits for an opportunity to go outside.*

**DAWN**   You have a good time?

**BILL**   Take it easy—

*Bill takes her arm and tries to walk her away from the building. She shakes him off.*

**DAWN**   Get offa me.

**BILL**   All I did was tell that guy to mind his own business.

**DAWN** *I* don't care what you're doin' up there—

**BILL** Well, maybe I'm nuts, but I do. I care what you think of me and it's pretty important to me that you believe me when I talk to you. OK? 'Cause I may do a lot of other things, but I care enough about your opinion of me that I don't want you to think I'm not being straight with you.

**DAWN** Straight with me!

**BILL** Dawn. I swear to God—I got no reason to bullshit you: So I don't know why I'm goin' through this with you, but my friend Jim lives upstairs with Amy Heinvald; it's her apartment—And that's all there is to it. I hardly even *know* Mrs. Heinvald, and anyway, she wasn't even *there* tonight. She's outta *town*. You don't want to believe me, there's nothin' I can say to you.

**DAWN** (*Slowly*) Well ... How come you were up there for so long?

**BILL** I didn't really think it was so long, but if you really want to know, I had to talk to Jim about something private which doesn't concern you and which I'm not at liberty to talk about with you. He's goin' through a hard time and some really weird, really upsetting shit, and I can't talk about it because it would be a breach of privacy. You don't want to believe me, there's nothing I can do.

**DAWN** I don't.

**BILL** All right. Only personally, I think that's a shame, because I really thought we really had something goin' between us. At least that's how I felt. I don't know: Maybe you didn't feel that way. So maybe it's for the best, you know? Because the way things have been goin' between us, I wouldn't know how else to stop it. It doesn't help that my wife and I are like—I don't even know what—like we don't even know each other any more. I respect her, she's my wife, she's the mother of my children, I'll never say a word against her as long as I live, but it's like we're strangers. And it's been like that for three years. If it wasn't for the kids, we wouldn't be together and that's the truth. You want me to be honest? I'll be honest: (*Pause*) This is very difficult for me to say. But I haven't felt like this about somebody since—I don't even know when. I don't know if I *ever* felt this way about somebody. It's new to me. And I'm scared. You know, I think I'm a little bit like you: I could walk into a room and face down twenty bad guys and I wouldn't blink an eye. But somethin' like this, and the whole world starts goin' around in my head. Because when I'm with you, I really feel like you are the real thing, and everything else seems like bullshit to me. You want me to be honest? That's as honest as I get.

*Jeff, having now edged his way to the door, pokes his head out.*

**JEFF**  Excuse me, Bill?

**BILL**  What.

**JEFF**  Um—Mrs. Heinvald just buzzed down. She says you left your hat upstairs and she wants to know if you want her to bring it down or if you want to pick it up tomorrow.

*Pause.*

**BILL**  You're a pip.

**JEFF**  I'm sorry—I—

**BILL**  (*Moving toward him*)  Get—back—

*Jeff goes inside. Pause.*

**BILL**  All right. I'm busted. I don't know what to say. I'm sorry.

**DAWN**  Yeah, right.

**BILL**  No, I'm sincere about that. I really am. But you gotta believe me, I mean—I don't know what's the matter with me. I really don't. It's like I'm a sex addict. I think I need help. I really do.

**DAWN**  Hey! How *stupid* do you think I *am*?

**BILL**  No, wait a minute—it's like, whenever I meet someone I could really care about, it's like I always gotta be doin' somethin' to mess it up, and I don't know why. You know? Why?

**DAWN**  Maybe it's because you're a dirty fuckin' liar.

**BILL**  Whoa, hey, Dawn: Slow down. OK? I'm just trying to talk to you—

**DAWN**  I know what you're tryin' to do and you can forget it. We're workin' together, let's work together—

**BILL**  —OK—

**DAWN**  —I don't care what you do up there, I don't care what you do period. I *told* you this was a bad idea—

**BILL**  OK. You wanna do it that way—?

**DAWN**  —only don't expect me to sit down here and *cover* for you when the dispatcher wants to know where you *went*. I signed up to be a cop, not lookout patrol at the whorehouse.

*Pause.*

**BILL**  OK, first of all, she's not a whore.

**DAWN**  Oh she's not?

**BILL**  It actually happens that the lady has a lot of class. So just be careful what you say about her.

**DAWN**  I don't *believe* this!

**BILL**  Second of all, I'm sorry if I hurt your feelings, but you don't come down here from the Police Academy in your little pigtails and tell me what to do. OK? I tell *you* what to do. And if I want you to sit down here and wait for me all night, that's exactly what you're gonna do, every *night* if I want you to—

**DAWN**  No I'm not—

**BILL**  Oh yes you are. You're gonna sit down here with *Jeff* and you're gonna answer the radio for me, and if you don't like it, Dawn, then—maybe you shouldn't be tryin' to be a cop. Because that's what cops do, is they support each other. They help each other, they're there for each other—and they don't judge each other and they don't fuck each other up. OK? So before you go cryin' home to your Mom and Dad how your partner was just mean to you, just remember I am not the one who put some drunk in the hospital last night for callin' me names.

**DAWN**  That's not what happened.

**BILL**  I don't care what happened. My *three*-year-old coulda handled that situation better than you, OK? So settle down because you're totally outta control. And the way you're acting now is completely unprofessional. Now, I'm gonna go up there and get my hat. And you're gonna wait down here till I come back.

**DAWN**  No I'm not.

**BILL**  Oh, you'll wait.

**DAWN**  No I won't.

**BILL**  All right. You wanna take off? Take off. Only see how you do in this Division without me backin' you up. See if

55

things are a little different for you from now on. Because one word from me and these guys'll make your life so miserable I couldn't even begin to describe it.

**DAWN** Look—Bill—I don't care about you and Mrs. Heinvald—

**BILL** (*Overlapping*) No—you made your choice—I'm tryin' to talk to you, you're givin' me all these ultimatums—!

**DAWN** (*Overlapping*) —I just wanna do my job.

**BILL** —That's OK: You made your choice. So see what happens when you come to work tomorrow. Go ahead.

**DAWN** Well—How do you think your friend Lieutenant Finelli's gonna like it if I tell him what you been doin' every night in the middle of your shift?

**BILL** Oh. All right. Thank you. Now I know where I stand. Before, I didn't realize. OK. Yeah: You could do that. You could do that right now. Only who do you think he's gonna believe? You or me? And second of all, see what happens at your hearing. See what I tell 'em in my report. "*I* didn't see him rush her . . ." That's all I gotta say. "I didn't see him rush her . . ." and that will be It For You, Good-bye. OK? And I don't know when they're gonna schedule that fuckin' thing, so if I were you I would be very, very *nice* to me for the next few months, Dawn. Oh, I don't appreciate havin' to have this kind of conversation. Uh, I got some flaws and that's the end of me. Not good enough, right? So take off. You're never gonna be a cop anyway. You're never gonna be anything. So go ahead. Take off.

*Bill goes inside the lobby, past Jeff, and off toward the elevators. The elevator dings. Dawn stays where she is. Jeff looks out at her. She won't look at him.*

# ACT TWO, SCENE ONE

*Late the next night. Jeff is watching William smoke a cigarette.
Silence.*

**JEFF**  Does it ever strike you as stupid that you're "the
Captain?"

**WILLIAM**  No.

**JEFF**  No—I don't mean—

**WILLIAM**  How do you mean?

**JEFF**  I don't mean "Don't you think it's stupid that you're
the *supervisor*." Obviously you're the *supervisor;* I just mean
don't you ever think it's stupid that you're *called* the
"*Captain?*"

**WILLIAM**  No, Jeff, I don't.

**JEFF**  But there's no other *ranks*.

**WILLIAM**  What?

**JEFF**  Well—Everybody else in the company is just a *guard,*
but you're "the Captain." Do you know what I mean?
Why aren't you a *corporal?* Why do they skip right up to
captain? Or why aren't you just "the supervisor?"

**WILLIAM**  Because this is a security company, Jeff.

**JEFF**  I know that—

**WILLIAM**  And occasionally some of the people who work for
this company do actually have to provide security for the
buildings we're working at.

**JEFF**  I know that—

**WILLIAM** All right—

**JEFF** —I do my bit.

**WILLIAM** Well . . . I don't think it's inappropriate for a semi-military organization to borrow a little military vernacular.

**JEFF** We're not a semi-military organization . . .

**WILLIAM** Semi-military, semi-police, whatever you want to call it.

**JEFF** I don't want to call it anything, I just—

**WILLIAM** It's not like anybody's calling me "captain" anyway, so what do you care about it?

**JEFF** I don't. I'm just making conversation.

**WILLIAM** Well, why you gotta be making conversation? I'm just trying to sit here for a minute. You feel like you gotta say stupid shit to me just because I'm in the Goddamn room, I'll be on my way and you can get back to your crossword puzzle.

**JEFF** What's the matter with you? Lighten up. I didn't say anything.

**WILLIAM** I'm sorry.

**JEFF** How's your brother doing?

*William does not respond.*

**JEFF** Well, I can see you probably don't want to talk about that. But I was thinking about it today, and I think . . . (*Off William's look:*) No, really. I was. And seriously, I don't mean to be—I'm not bein' cavalier about it. But I was thinking about it and I really think when you talk to the cops you should probably just go in there and tell the truth.

Because—I realize you probably don't care what I think . . . but you did ask me my opinion last night, and I realize I wasn't very helpful, so I thought about it some more today and that's really what I think that you should do. For what it's worth. I know you probably don't even want to hear it . . . But I just want you to know, you don't have to worry about me. I mean . . . you took me into your confidence and I really appreciated that . . . 'cause it made me feel like you considered me as a friend. (*Pause*) You're not sorry you told me about it, are you?

**WILLIAM**   Yeah, Jeff, I'm a little sorry.

**JEFF**   Come on, man. You can trust me. What am I gonna do? I'm not gonna say anything.

**WILLIAM**   OK, Jeff. My brother's had a rough time. And he just doesn't have the strength of character to meet a lot of the situations he's found himself in. Which is no excuse . . . But he didn't create those situations either. And I'm a great believer in personal responsibility—as you know—

**JEFF**   Yes, yes, I know.

**WILLIAM**   . . . so I don't usually like to say this, but sometimes I think he just never had a chance, because he has a very average personality. Now, I'm very disciplined. But that's just my nature. I was always that way. So when all these criminals used to come around our house and try to tempt me, I would stay away. But I can't take a lot of credit for that, 'cause I was just a little kid. So how am I gonna be patting myself on the back for how I acted or didn't act when I was ten years old? That's just absurd. But he was more like a regular kid. So he got sucked up by these criminals and that was it. If they hadn't been around he would have been a so-called normal kid and now he'd be a so-called normal man, probably inflicting lawful misery on someone in the corporate world, or what have you. But I'm just exhausted with it, I really am.

**JEFF**   You must be.

**WILLIAM**   At any rate . . . I guess that's neither here nor there.

**JEFF**   When do you have to talk to the cops?

**WILLIAM**   Yeah—I already talked to them. I t—I spoke to them this morning.

**JEFF**   You did? Wow, I didn't realize that. So how did that go?

**WILLIAM**   It went fine, Jeff.

**JEFF**   Did you talk to your brother?

**WILLIAM**   No, but I spoke with his attorney. Which was very interesting. And he threw kind of a whole new light on the situation for me.

**JEFF**   Oh yeah? What did he say?

**WILLIAM**   Well, he said a lot of things, but I had a hard time following most of it because for the first fifteen minutes of the conversation he had my brother mixed up with another case.

**JEFF**   Are you kidding me?

**WILLIAM**   No. Didn't know my name, didn't know my brother's name—And then he's like, "Oh, oh, you're *that* case, oh OK." So after that I kinda lost track of some of the details of the defense he was outlining for me.

**JEFF**   Are you kidding?

**WILLIAM**   No. Then I went and talked to these two detectives for about, oh, I don't know, two and a half hours, something like that. Then I went home, called my parents, talked to my mother for a while, talked to my father for about five minutes. Talked to my wife, fended off *her* questions. Had to have a brief discussion about our relationship. Called my Uncle Paul, talked to him for a while. Then I took about a three-minute bath, ate some dinner, put on my uniform, came to work, and now I'm here. And Jeff, I'm glad to be here. Because believe it or not, I find your presence to be very soothing. You're probably the most easygoing person I've spoken to all day. Probably the most easygoing person I know. Which most of the time I find to be somewhat irritating, to tell you the truth, but right now I find it very calming.

**JEFF**  I'm glad you're here too, man. (*Pause*) So, but, I mean, but, like, what did you tell them?

*Pause.*

**WILLIAM**  I—told them I was at the movies.

**JEFF**  Well, but—I mean—So—You don't think—Now you think your brother didn't do it? Or—

**WILLIAM**  I know he didn't do it because I was at the movies with him. All right?

**JEFF**  Yeah—No—I understand—

**WILLIAM**  Understand what? What do you understand?

**JEFF**  I understand you were at the movies with him.

**WILLIAM**  That's right.

**JEFF**  OK. (*Pause*) No, it's just that—

**WILLIAM**  It's just what? (*Pause*) What? Do you have something you want to say to me?

61

**JEFF**  No—

**WILLIAM**  You have some helpful suggestions for me?

**JEFF**  No—

**WILLIAM**  I know you don't.

**JEFF**  All right.

**WILLIAM**  I know it's all right.

**JEFF**  No. I just—William, I just—I don't know: I don't like saying this, William . . . But I feel like it's my civic duty—

**WILLIAM**  Your what?

**JEFF**  No—

**WILLIAM**  Since when do you have a sense of civic duty, Jeff?

**JEFF**  OK, not my civic duty—

**WILLIAM**  Since when do you have a sense of duty period?

**JEFF**  I have a sense of duty. (*Pause*) I just—you know . . . What if he really did it?

**WILLIAM**  What do you mean, "What if he did it?" I was at the movies with him.

**JEFF**  Yeah. All right.

**WILLIAM**  They want to *prove* he did it, let them *prove* it! I can't participate in this. I'll participate in a fair trial . . . I can't participate in this!

**JEFF**  Yeah! No! I mean—

**WILLIAM**  I mean you hear about this shit all the time; you hear about guys who go to jail because their lawyer was asleep in court, or because they forgot to file some deposition or something because they have two hundred cases apiece and about five minutes for each one. And then these cops pull you in the room and you gotta make up your mind then and there what you're going to say, and I don't know if he did it or not but I just—I couldn't do it to him, Jeff. My whole life I've told the truth, I always tell the truth. Because I believe in that, OK? You don't worry about if the world is bad or good, because I know Goddamn well it's bad. You just do your best and let the chips fall where they may. But I couldn't do it to him, Jeff, I just couldn't do it. And you don't have to ask me "What if he did it," because that's all I can fuckin' think about!

**JEFF**  I know, I wouldn't know what to do either! I probably would have done the exact same thing.

*Pause.*

**WILLIAM**  I'm sorry. I apologize.

**JEFF**  You don't have to apologize . . .

**WILLIAM**  Anyway, so then I ran into Big Bill and he just asks me straight out, you know, if it was true—so I told him, "Yeah, Bill, it's true." And he looks at me, real tough and what have you, and he says, "Don't bullshit me, William," and I said, "Bill, I'm not," and then he just sat back and he said, "OK, man, I believe you."

**JEFF**  What's he got to do with it?

**WILLIAM**  Nothing. He was just there—I guess—'Cause he knows me . . .

**JEFF**  Well . . . What if you—I don't know . . . What if you—

**WILLIAM**  See, I was thinking—I was talking to my Uncle Paul—You've heard me mention him—

**JEFF**  Sure. You talk about him all the time—

**WILLIAM**  (*On "all"*) All right, well, I was talking to him, and he was saying how we should put our heads together and just try to find a decent lawyer to take my brother's case. Scrape together some money, or find somebody who'd want to take the case pro bono. But he assumes that I was with him . . . They all assume . . . They don't understand. (*Pause*) But if we had a halfway decent lawyer, somehow, then I could probably feel more confident just letting things take their own course.

**JEFF**  That sounds better to me. I think that's a really good idea.

**WILLIAM**  Anyway . . . We probably shouldn't talk about this too much more . . .

**JEFF**  Well . . . I mean . . . we already have. So . . .

**WILLIAM**  I know, but . . . Well, if by any chance anybody does ask you about it . . . you just hold off. If you're comfortable doing that. I talked to you about this and I shouldn't have. That's not your fault. That's my fault—But I still need a little time to try to find him a decent lawyer, so at least he has a chance.

*Bill and Dawn have entered onto the street. They come into the lobby.*

**BILL**  Good evening, gentlemen.

**WILLIAM**  Hello Bill.

**BILL**  Hey, buddy. How's it goin'?

**WILLIAM**  OK. How are you?

**BILL**  I'm OK. You mind if I talk to you for a second?

**WILLIAM**  No, not at all.

**BILL**  Would you excuse us for a second please, Jeff?

**JEFF**  Um—Sure . . .

*Bill takes William aside. Jeff drifts toward Dawn.*

**JEFF**  How you doin'?

**DAWN**  Fine.

**BILL**  (*To William, aside*)  So listen—I think you're gonna get
some interesting news tomorrow. I talked to the detectives
after you left, I told 'em I knew you, told 'em I believed
you . . . I even—this'll amuse you, actually, I even went to
the ADA's office and I told him I would vouch for you—
This guy was not exactly thrilled to see me either, believe
me. They don't exactly like strange cops walkin' into their
offices and tellin' 'em who to charge and who not to
charge, but I figure what the hell. Somebody doesn't stick
up for your brother they're gonna lock him up with some
*really* unpleasant characters and that's gonna be *it* for him.

**WILLIAM**  I really appreciate that, Bill. I just hope—

**BILL**  (*On 2nd "I"*)  Naw, don't worry about that: I just think
that what you and your brother both gotta think about is if he
*didn't* have an alibi, or if I didn't know you: You think about
this kid's character and you think, "I could see him doin'
somethin' like that someday." So if not this time, when?

**WILLIAM**  I know, Bill. It—I know.

**BILL**  Just somethin' to chew on. OK, buddy. I'll see you
later. (*Calling out*) Uh, Jeff, I'll be goin' up to 22–J. That's
22–J.

**JEFF**  Would you mind signing in? (*Off Bill's look*) Never mind. I'll do it.

*Bill exits toward the elevators. Jeff signs him in.*

**WILLIAM**  I'll see you later, Jeff.

**JEFF** (*Sotto voce*)  Hey, wait, so what did he *say*?

**WILLIAM**  I'll tell you about it later.

**JEFF**  Sure. If you wanna come by when you're done with your rounds . . .

**WILLIAM**  Yeah, maybe I will.

**JEFF**  But is everything OK? What happened?

**WILLIAM**  I'll tell you *later*, Jeff.

*William goes onto the street and exits. Jeff and Dawn are alone.*

**JEFF** (*Pointedly letting her know he knows her name*)  How's it goin'—Dawn?

**DAWN**  Fine.

*Pause.*

**JEFF**  So is he doing this just to torture you now?

**DAWN**  He's showin' me who's boss.

**JEFF**  Which would be—him, right? I assume?

**DAWN**  I guess so.

**JEFF**  Well . . . Your turn will come. Someday you'll be upstairs havin' sex with some guy, and your rookie partner'll be downstairs learnin' who's boss from you . . . I'm sorry. Seriously though, how are things goin' down at the station? Pretty tough?

**DAWN**  No. I don't care if people know about my private
business. That's their problem if they think it's interesting . . .

**JEFF**  Hm.

**DAWN**  What really bothers me is the illegality of this.

**JEFF**  Of course.

**DAWN**  Do you *know* how much trouble he would be in if I
*told* anybody about this?

**JEFF**  So why don't you say something?

**DAWN**  Believe me. You just don't do that. Now could we
change the subject?

**JEFF**  Sure. Sorry . . . How's that guy you beat up? I'm sorry.

**DAWN**  That's OK. They think he's gonna lose his eye.

**JEFF**  Are you kidding?

**DAWN**  No.

**JEFF**  Why?

**DAWN**  Because I *hit* him in it, that's why. So now they think
he's gonna lose the eye, or go blind in it, and him and his
wife are suing me, the Police Department, and practically
everybody who ever worked for the City of New York. He
was totally chargin' me, he weighed about five hundred
pounds, and he was drunk out of his mind. But who cares
about *that,* right?

**JEFF**  But they can't win, though . . .

**DAWN**  If nobody backs me up they can.

*Pause.*

**JEFF**  How long have you been on the Force now?

**DAWN**  Three months.

**JEFF**  You've racked up quite a few accomplishments in a short time.

**DAWN**  I know, right?

**JEFF**  Well . . . You missed a really great game today . . .

**DAWN**  Oh yeah?

**JEFF**  Actually it was only so-so. They fell apart in the second half.

**DAWN**  Yeah. I watched some of it on TV . . .

**JEFF**  I thought you didn't like basketball.

**DAWN**  I don't. My father had it on.

**JEFF**  Oh, do you live with them?

**DAWN**  Who, my parents? No. *No* . . . I was just visiting. (*Pause*) I looked for you in the crowd on TV, but they didn't show you.

**JEFF**  Yeah, I told 'em to stop filming me all the time. You know? People want to see the *game*. They're sick of watching me all the time. "How did Jeff react to that play? What did Jeff think of that call?" It's enough already.

**DAWN**  (*Smiling*)  Yeah . . . ?

**JEFF**  To tell you the truth I couldn't really concentrate on it too well. I can't really concentrate on anything so well lately. I guess my mind is too distracted.

**DAWN**  Oh yeah?

68

**JEFF**  Yeah, I been very—my best friend is getting married on Saturday—my friend Scott—and I'm supposed to organize this bachelor party . . . so that's been a big pain in the ass.

**DAWN**  What are you gonna go to a topless place or something?

**JEFF**  Who knows? I hate bachelor parties. Bunch of guys sitting around some apartment drinking beer and watching porno movies—it makes me sick, it really just disgusts me.

**DAWN**  I thought all guys liked porno movies.

**JEFF**  Well, we do. It's just the thought of all these guys together, sitting around doing this stuff that makes me uncomfortable.

**DAWN**  What do you mean?

**JEFF**  I don't know. I just don't like it. Like I don't like the way groups of guys—the way men behave in a group. Like the way some guys get when they think they're playing sports. Or pretty much any bunch of guys anywhere making loud noises and screaming and impressing each other with what a bunch of morons they are. I really don't like it. It makes me sick.

**DAWN**  You'd love the Police Force.

**JEFF**  No, I don't think I would. (*Pause*) Hey, did I tell you I saw a really nice apartment today? See, I've been—I live with my brother Marty—I didn't tell you about this?

**DAWN**  No.

**JEFF**  Well, I live with my brother Marty and his wife and two kids, in Astoria. (*Pause*) I rent a room from them. (*Pause*) And they're great, but now that I'm gettin' back on my feet a little bit, I've been thinking I really want to get my own place. So

69

today I saw a place that seems really nice, so if everything
goes well I think I'm gonna be able to move in the first of
the month, which is gonna be—amazing. My own little
kitchen . . . Do you like to cook at all?

**DAWN**  Not really, not that much.

**JEFF**  Yeah, I really enjoy cooking.

**DAWN**  My mother's a good cook. Really good . . . Only it's
not like it's free . . . You know?

**JEFF**  No, what do you mean?

**DAWN**  No, it's just always like, "Gee Ma, is there anything
about my life I'm doin' *right*?"

**JEFF**  Oh, really?

**DAWN**  . . . She's always making these little comments . . .

**JEFF**  That's too bad . . .

**DAWN**  Oh but not just to me: to everyone. Like, there's
always something wrong with every little thing you do. She
has all these little ways of puttin' everybody down. And
then she's miserable because nobody wants to hang around
her. I swear to God she's nuts.

**JEFF**  Yeah, my old man was very—

**DAWN**  And my Dad just sits there, right? Like nothin's
bothering him, right?

**JEFF**  Uh-huh?

**DAWN**  And she's sittin' there makin' all these little backhand
remarks about everybody: about his mother and father, and
everybody in his family, about his personal habits, right?

**JEFF**  Uh-huh?

**DAWN**  And he just lets it wash over him, like he doesn't even hear it. And I asked him, I said, "How can you listen to that shit all day long?" And he says, "Listen to what? What am I gonna do, get divorced? Let her make herself miserable, I can't stop her. I just think about other things when she's talking."

**JEFF**  See—That is the great attitude to have.

**DAWN**  I sure don't have it.

**JEFF**  No, me neither. But I can really relate to that because my old man was a little bit like that, too—

**DAWN**  What do you mean, like puttin' everybody down . . . ?

**JEFF**  Not putting people down exactly, but just very very hard to get along with.

**DAWN**  Uh-huh . . .

**JEFF**  And I'll tell you something: I really used to resent it—

**DAWN**  You're Goddamn right you resent it.

**JEFF**  Yeah, only except now that he's gone, and I don't have to listen to it anymore, you start to reevaluate things a little bit. Like he had a lot of really good qualities I think I could really learn from. And just in general, there's a lot of things I admire about his whole *generation* . . .

**DAWN**  Oh, definitely . . .

**JEFF**  Like he was tough. I mean he was *really* tough. And when he said he was gonna do something, he did it. He didn't just talk. Which is fortunate in a way, for everyone, because when he talked he didn't actually make a lot of fucking sense, if you know what I mean. I mean his opinions were pretty undeveloped, you know? But you have to admire that kind of character.

**DAWN**  Definitely. Definitely.

**JEFF**  My goal is to acquire that type of backbone and that kind of self-assurance without becoming as ossified as that. You know what I mean? Like, can you inspire that kind of admiration in people and really stand up for what you believe in, and still be like an open-minded person? That's my question.

| JEFF | DAWN |
|------|------|
| But like— | I don't know. I know |
| I'm sorry— | people who— |
| I didn't mean to interrupt— | That's all right. No, go ahead. I don't even know what I was gonna say. |

**JEFF**  No, I was just gonna say . . . I was gonna say . . . Well, I had some really interesting thing I was gonna say, but now I forgot.

**DAWN**  That's OK. You don't have to be interesting all the time. I'll still like you.

*Jeff is momentarily embarrassed.*

**JEFF**  Anywa . . . Anyway . . . What I was gonna say . . . I was *gonna* say, I think that's—for some people that's a form of *weak*ness . . .

*Pause.*

**DAWN**  (*Not following*)  What . . . is?

**JEFF**  No—yeah—I mean in another way—For other people—if you look at it another way—Take your partner, for example.

**DAWN**  What about him?

**JEFF**  Nothing. He's just very self-assured, obviously, but he's also like a total scumbag and I'm just wondering if you can have one without the other. You know what I mean? (*Pause*) Anyway . . . Maybe you don't want to talk about that right now.

**DAWN**  I don't care. . . . Must be nice to have it all be a theory.

**JEFF**  What do you mean?

**DAWN**  I mean it must be nice to sit here and watch other people gettin' squeezed to death by their own dumb-ass mistakes and sit around and think about how interesting it is.

**JEFF**  It's not all theoretical to me. Don't be like your mother.

**DAWN**  I'm not like my *mother* . . . !

| **JEFF** | |
|---|---|
| I'm just a very empathetic person, and to tell you the God's honest truth, Dawn, I feel a little bit responsible for the mess you're in. Because if I would've— | **DAWN** You're not responsible. *I'm* responsible. I'm *totally* responsible. |

**JEFF**  Yeah, but if I would have kept my big mouth shut, it probably never would have escalated to this point. I just hate to see guys like that get away with stuff like that, because that's the kind of stuff that *I* wanna get away with only I can't figure out how it's done.

**DAWN**  That's how you wanna be? You wanna be like him?

**JEFF**  No, not exactly, but yeah, in a way. The guy has no qualms about anything, he does whatever he wants, he gets everything he wants, and as far as I can see he feels just fine about it. So yeah, I wouldn't mind being a little bit like that, would you?

**DAWN**  I don't *know* . . . ! I don't wanna *talk* about this. Do you have any idea what I been *goin'* through . . . ?

**JEFF**  OK, you're right, I'm sorry.

**DAWN**  I don't know what I'm gonna do. He's gonna come back down in a few minutes—I don't know what to do. I don't know what he wants from me. All I did was tell him I don't wanna wait down here while he's upstairs with her when he's supposed to be working and he went fuckin' nuts. I don't know what to do.

**JEFF**  What can you do?

**DAWN**  I don't know. Maybe he won't go through with it.

**JEFF**  Through with what? (*Pause*) Go through with what?

**DAWN**  He said . . .

*Pause.*

**JEFF**  What?

**DAWN**  He said he's gonna get me kicked off the Force unless I'm really "nice" to him.

**JEFF**  Nice . . . *Nice,* nice? Or—What does he mean?

**DAWN**  Uh, gee, Jeff, I don't know. What do you think he means?

**JEFF**  Are you serious?

**DAWN**  Oh yeah, we got a big date after work tonight.

**JEFF**  But isn't that like, sexual harassment or something?

**DAWN**  Uh, no, actually, I think it's called rape.

**JEFF**  Rape?

**DAWN**  Rape, sexual coercion . . . I don't know what it's called.

**JEFF**  What do you mean you don't know what it's called? You're a cop: Aren't you supposed to know the names of all the different crimes?

**DAWN**  Jesus Christ, what difference does it make?

**JEFF**
Yeah, but can't you *tell*
somebody about this? Don't        **DAWN**
they have some committee           Uh, yeah, only I don't think
or something you can talk to?       they'd be too sympathetic.

**JEFF**  Why not?

**DAWN**  Because I was already *with* him, Jeff. And everybody knows about it. OK? So two days later I'm gonna turn around and complain about it?

**JEFF**  But God *damn!*

**DAWN**  What's the big deal? I got myself into this. Now I'm in it. Maybe he won't go through with it. You know? Maybe he'll be too tired. I still can't believe he would do something like that. But let's face it, I gotta be the worst judge of character in the history of the fuckin' Earth. I mean can you believe this shit? Three days ago I'm practically in love with the guy and now he's tellin' me—Well, that is not gonna happen. I don't know what's gonna happen when it doesn't, but that is not happening. Let him get me kicked off the Force. Let him try. It's not worth it. I'm not gonna be one of those, "Oh yeah, I let him rape me because I didn't know what else to do . . ." I'd rather be *dead*, OK? But I gotta find some way outta this, man. I don't know what I'm gonna do, but I gotta do something. I just gotta figure out what it is.

**JEFF**   I wish I could do something to help you.

**DAWN**   Yeah, so do I. That's all right. I gotta calm down . . . (*Pause*) Did your friend William tell you what happened to his brother?

*Pause.*

**JEFF**   He told me his brother was arrested.

**DAWN**   Nice, huh?

**JEFF**   It's terrible.

**DAWN**   I don't know, Jeff . . . You just can't believe some of the people in this world. You know? You can't even believe what they do to each other. And I only been doin' this for three months.

**JEFF**   Well . . . at least you can do something about it. You know? I mean, at least you can, like, help them, sometimes.

**DAWN**   Yeah, well, that's what they tell you. But it really depends on . . . Depends on a lot of things. Depends on who you're working with, for one thing. That's what's so crazy about this thing with Bill.

**JEFF**   How do you mean?

**DAWN**   Because the guy is supposedly like this genius cop. Like he just got on the list to get a gold shield? (*Explaining*) You know: to be a detective?

**JEFF**  Yeah, I know. I watch TV.

**DAWN**  All right, but that's not so easy if you didn't go through Narcotics or some of the other branches. He's always goin' out of his way. Like this thing with your friend's brother? Bill totally diffused that whole thing. He didn't have to do that. That's not even his case. Everybody's talkin' about it.

**JEFF**  Yeah. (*Pause*) How do you mean he diffused it?

**DAWN**  Well—you know—'cause they were ready to hang this kid . . . I just hope he's *right,* you know?

**JEFF**  Yeah. What do you mean?

**DAWN**  I hope he's right, because if he's not, he's helpin' this kid get away with murder.

**JEFF**  So, but—So—I don't understand. What happened? Now they're gonna release him?

**DAWN**  Yeah, supposedly.

**JEFF**  Why would they do that?

**DAWN**  (*Confused*)  Because his alibi checked out. Because your friend was with him on the night in question. Or so he said. Why? You know somethin' about it they don't?

**JEFF**  No. I don't know anything about it. We didn't talk about it. You know, he just told me, you know, that he heard his brother was arrested . . .

**DAWN**  Oh.

**JEFF**  . . . he didn't tell me any of the details. (*Pause*) So do they just *release* the guy if Bill tells 'em to? That doesn't seem very systematic.

**DAWN**   No, no, they obviously don't do that: They ask you a million questions, especially a family member. But they obviously believed him. And Bill believes him. And that definitely helps . . . And this one was horrible. You know they *all* raped her, they beat her up so bad her own best friend couldn't ID the body, and then they stuffed her in the closet and just let her die.

**JEFF**   Yeah. Jesus Christ.

**DAWN**   You know she had three kids?

**JEFF**   Yeah . . . I overheard Bill sayin' something about that.

**DAWN**   What are they supposed to do now, you know?

**JEFF**   What will they do?

**DAWN**   Far as I know they're all goin' to Social Services. There was no other relatives.

*Jeff does not respond.*

**DAWN**   Want to know what *else* happened in the neighborhood this week? 'Cause I can just go down the list.

**JEFF**   No thanks.

**DAWN**   They say summer's when it really gets bad. At least that's what everybody's telling me. So I can't wait for that . . . If I last that long.

**JEFF**   You will.

**DAWN**   But I'll tell you something, Jeff: Whoever did that, if just once in a while I could have something to do with catching somebody like that, making sure they could get what they deserve, I would definitely feel like my life was well spent. You know?

**JEFF**   Yeah . . . It's weird . . . Like, I watch you guys goin' back and forth and it's . . . I don't know. I gotta get out of this situation. I just—

**DAWN**   What situation?

**JEFF**   This *job* situation. I think it's startin' to drive me crazy. I know you're having some problems at work right now—

**DAWN**   Uh, slightly.

**JEFF**   Well, OK, but at least you're *doing* something. You're trying to *do* something important with your *life*. But I got no family, I got . . . I don't know. I just feel like I want to do something. To help somebody. Or do something. Contribute. I don't know. Work with kids. Or—I mean, I don't particularly *like* kids, but you know what I mean.

**DAWN**   Well—There's all kinds of ways to be useful. It doesn't have to be your life's work.

**JEFF**   Yeah, but that's what I'm saying, that's what's so great about you guys is that it *is* your life's work. It's your *life's work*. It's not just your spare time . . . And that's—It just makes me think that's the kind of thing that I would like to do . . . See, I always thought I'd just be a Navy guy, because of my Dad . . . And that would be something: You know: Defend the country . . . But I couldn't stand it. Too many guys. All around. Guys guys guys. Groups of guys. That is not for me.

**DAWN**   Yeah, I remember you were tellin' me about that . . .

**JEFF**   No way, not for me.

**DAWN**   Yeah, I think maybe you got a little thing about that? Like a psychological fixation or something you might wanna look into.

**JEFF** I don't want to look into anything, I just don't wanna be around a bunch of screamin' guys.

**DAWN** Well . . . Thanks for sayin' all that.

**JEFF** Oh. That's all right. I mean, you're welcome.

**DAWN** No seriously, I really need to hear that kinda thing right now . . .

**JEFF** And I know you're havin' a hard time now, but I want you to know, I really admire you . . . Even though you're havin' trouble . . . I feel like it's inspiring to me, to see somebody goin' through all that stuff because they want to do something to make a contribution.

**DAWN** Thank you . . . !

**JEFF** Friends?

**DAWN** Definitely.

*Pause.*

**JEFF** So listen: I have a hypothetical situation I want to ask you about.

**DAWN** OK.

**JEFF** This whole thing with William kind of reminds me of this, so I wanted to ask you . . . Suppose you have a friend, and a close relative of his is arrested for a very serious crime . . .

**DAWN** Yeah?

*Long pause.*

**JEFF** So a close relative of his is arrested for a serious crime, and that relative is using your friend as an alibi—like William's brother did, only in this case it's not really true:

Your friend was *not* with the relative at the time of the crime. But that doesn't mean the guy *did* it; it just means he doesn't have a good alibi, and he's worried he's gonna go to jail. Are you with me?

**DAWN**  Yeah . . . ?

**JEFF**  Now, ordinarily your friend is a very upright kind of a guy. Again, kind of like William, but hypothetical— somebody who would never ordinarily lie for this relative. But he doesn't know if his relative is guilty or if it's a frame-up or what. And then he meets the relative's *lawyer,* and it's one of those court-appointed lawyers, and the lawyer is just completely incompetent and out of it, like he's drunk, and he doesn't know the client's name, and can't remember any of the details of the case . . . Like you might as well not even *have* a lawyer, this guy is so bad . . . Are you following me?

**DAWN**  I'm following you.

**JEFF**  So *now,* my friend—hypothetically—he starts talking to the cops, and without realizing it, he's backing up his brother's story because he just can't bring himself to just throw his brother—his relative, whatever—to the wolves, and on the strength of his interview, or for whatever reason, the detectives decide the relative is a solid citizen and the charges won't stand up in court and they decide to release him. OK? A lot of similarities to the William thing.

**DAWN**  What's your question?

**JEFF**  My *question* is—How is anybody supposed to expect the brother—my friend, my imaginary friend or whatever—not to back up his relative's story? Considering that he's a human being and he has feelings, and no matter what he thinks the right thing to do is, he's gotta answer to their parents and all the rest of it. And by the same token, what do you think—My question is: What if *I*—me—*I* know the story is bullshit because my friend told me so, but nobody even knows I know anything. This is all for an idea for a novel I have, see. And for the character that would be me, see, I'm not sure what he should do. It's not *his* brother— *my* brother. But now the relative is being released and potentially he's a murderer, but there's no way to tell.

**DAWN**  Well . . . that's why they have such a thing as trial by jury, Jeff.

**JEFF**  Yeah, but they *don't,* because the lawyer is no good.

**DAWN**  Then you do something about *that*. But you can't just lie to the police.

**JEFF**  OK, good, that's good. Like what?

**DAWN**  Well, you can ask for a different lawyer, if the guy was really drunk; you can try askin' the judge—

**JEFF**  But, OK, but what if he wasn't literally drunk? What if I just said that as an extreme—

**DAWN**  If he wasn't drunk, or you can't prove he was drunk or something really serious like that, they're probably *not* gonna give you another one because they have no *reason* to give you another one. They don't offer you a *selection*. If you can't afford a lawyer they appoint a lawyer. Period. So—

**JEFF**  But then why should my friend tell the truth? Or why should I?

**DAWN**  Because you have to, that's all. Because there's no other way to do it. It's not your responsibility—

**JEFF**  It *is* my responsibility, it's *somebody's* responsibility—

**DAWN**  It's your responsibility to tell the truth—

**JEFF**  Why? If the city doesn't care about *its* responsibility to provide a decent defense—

**DAWN**  Because the city didn't *deliberately* give him a shitty lawyer. That's just an individual flaw in the system—

**JEFF**
It's *not* just a flaw in the system, it happens all the time; it happens *all* the time, unless you have a lot of money and you can afford your own lawyer—

**DAWN**
But it's still your responsibility to tell the truth and obey the law. You can't just make it *up* when there's some part of it that you don't like. You can appeal the decision, you can—

But somebody made up the *law,* didn't they? Some *people* made up the law. A bunch of people like you and me literally sat down and wrote it up and made up a salary for the court attorneys that wasn't very high, and made up rules about whether you were allowed to switch lawyers if the guy was no good— *God* didn't make up the rules—

Yeah, and if you don't like the—

Yeah, and if you don't like the rule, you can appeal the decision, or you could run for office, I guess, and try to change the law. Or you could vote for somebody you think

But by the time I do that my friend's relative is

gonna be getting stabbed
and raped in jail and maybe
he didn't *do* anything because
he didn't get a fair trial!

would do it better, or a
lot of things. But you
can't just go in and lie
about a murder trial!

**DAWN**   I don't know what to tell you, Jeff. You can't just lie
to the police. I don't know why. You can't.

**JEFF**   What if we lived in Nazi Germany? Could you lie to
the police then?

**DAWN**   We don't live in Nazi Germany!

**JEFF**   *We* don't live in Nazi Germany, but what if we did?
Would you still say you have to obey the law—?

**DAWN**   It's not the same as Nazi Germany!

**JEFF**
It's not the same in *theory*,
but if you look at the
statistics of who gets
arrested and who goes
to jail and who gets
sentenced to the death
penalty—what do you
mean "come on?"

**DAWN**
Oh come on!

**DAWN**   Well, if you think it's so unfair then why are you
tellin' me about it?

*Pause.*

**JEFF**
I'm not telling you about
anything! I'm outlining a
hypothetical situation

**DAWN**
Why are you tellin' me
about it?

84

for this thing I was gonna
write. Try to write.

**DAWN**  It bears a really suspicious resemblance to your friend
and his brother, don't you think?

**JEFF**  Just in general. The details are all different—Like I
added the thing about me knowing something about it . . .
The guy isn't a security guard, they weren't at the movies.
It's very different in the details. All I did was outline a
hypothetical situation.

*Long pause.*

**DAWN**  What do you mean they weren't at the movies?

**JEFF**  No—I mean—In my hypothetical . . . thing, nobody
was at the movies.

*Pause.*

**DAWN**  Oh, you mean because William and his brother were
supposedly at the movies?

**JEFF**  Yeah.

**DAWN**  I thought you said he didn't tell you about it.

*Pause.*

**JEFF**  Thought I said—I'm sorry. I'm confused. Thought who
said they didn't tell me about what?

**DAWN**  I thought you said William didn't tell you about it.

**JEFF**  He didn't.

**DAWN**  Then how did you know they were at the movies?

**JEFF**  Well—He told me *that*.

**DAWN**  What.

**JEFF**  Told me—This is so stupid. I was just outlining a hypothetical situation based on what William . . . This is really stupid.

**DAWN**  That's OK. Told you what?

**JEFF**  Told me—He told me that he heard his brother was arrested . . . And that it was something—I don't remember—Like for something that happened some night they were at the movies . . . And that it was really fucked up, and he knows his brother's done a lot of bad stuff, but he knows he didn't do this because he was at the movies with him.

**DAWN**  But then why'd you tell me that he didn't talk about it?

**JEFF**  Well, that was it. (*Pause*) What I said just then. (*Pause*) I wouldn't call that "talking" about it, but maybe that's just a difference of words . . . He didn't *really* talk about it. He didn't talk about it at great length, the way I probably would, or like your partner would, because we're more long-winded. But he told me what I told you.

**DAWN**  Which is what.

**JEFF**  That—you know—his brother was in trouble.

**DAWN**  OK, Jeff? If you know anything about this, you gotta tell me, and I mean right *now*.

**JEFF**  But I don't know anything, Dawn. I know I sound like I'm lying, but that's just because—It's that thing where if somebody thinks you're lying, even though you're not, you start to feel guilty like you're lying even though you're not? (*Pause*) It's like that.

**DAWN**  OK . . . I don't believe you, Jeff. So, um, I'm gonna go tell the detectives I think you know something and you can talk to *them*.

**JEFF**  No, don't do that, I don't know anything, you're just making me nervous—

**DAWN**  Hey! They're gonna release that kid tomorrow *morning*. And if he had anything to do with murdering that nurse that's gonna be on *your* conscience. And if *I* can tell you're lying, those detectives are gonna rip you to fuckin' pieces, OK?

**JEFF**  But I'm not, Dawn, I'm not.

**DAWN**  Do you wanna see what they did to that woman? You wanna come down to the station and look at the pictures?

**JEFF**  No, not really.

**DAWN**  Read your paper! It's on page twenty!

**JEFF**  I don't need to read it. I already read it.

*Pause.*

**DAWN** (*Softer*)  Come on, Jeff. Nobody's gonna blame him for trying to protect his brother. But—I mean—You don't want to be helping somebody get away with *murder,* Jeff. Like a real *murder* . . .

**JEFF**  I'm not.

**DAWN**  Do you?

**JEFF**  No. But I'm not.

**DAWN**  . . . Just tell the truth. That's all. That's all you gotta do. Just—truthfully—just tell me what he said.

**JEFF**  But I can't—I don't know anything. Honestly.

**DAWN**  Hey . . . I understand if you don't want to be goin' against your friend . . . And I know he's your boss. But that woman had friends too. She had three little kids. Now why is your friend and his brother more important than them?

*Jeff does not respond.*

**DAWN**  And I also—I just wanna tell you, we can totally try to keep you out of it. Whatever you tell me, I can take it right to the detectives. They could just use it as background information. You understand? They're still gonna have to substantiate it . . .

**JEFF**  You just said they were ready to hang him.

**DAWN**  OK, I know I said that. But they still gotta place him at the hospital. And Jeff, if he wasn't at the movies then he probably *did* fuckin' do it. All I'm sayin' is you gotta say whatever you know, regardless. That's just *basic*. And if they can place him at the hospital anyway, there's a really good chance we could keep you totally in the background. I mean, I probably couldn't promise that, but you got my word, we could definitely try.

*Jeff shakes his head.*

**DAWN**  Hey, Jeff. I really believed you when you said all that stuff about wantin' to do something. Don't you think that lady's kids deserve for you to tell the truth? You want to make a contribution, Jeff, here's your big chance.

*Pause.*

**JEFF**  Well—He, uh . . . Well . . . I don't think they were at the movies . . .

**DAWN**  OK. Why not?

88

**JEFF** Because he said—'Cause he said he wasn't.

**DAWN** OK, just tell me exactly what he said.

**JEFF** He said he heard his brother was arrested—

**DAWN** From who?

**JEFF** From his brother's girlfriend . . .

**DAWN** Did she say he *did* it?

**JEFF** No. No. Definitely not.

**DAWN** Are you sure?

**JEFF** Yes, definitely.

**DAWN** But he definitely wasn't at the movies.

**JEFF** No. Not with William.

**DAWN** And when did this all take place?

**JEFF** Last night.

**DAWN** OK.

**JEFF** The *conversation* took place last night.

**DAWN** I understand . . . (*Smiling*) OK . . .

**JEFF** What are you *smiling* about?

**DAWN** Nothing. It's—I'm not.

**JEFF** And then just now he came in and he told me that his brother's lawyer was such a bum he didn't know what to do, so that's why he told the detectives or the cops or whatever that they were at the movies.

*William enters onto the street.*

**DAWN** OK. Great. (*Seeing William*) All right. I'm, uh, I'm gonna—As soon as the detectives get to work, I'm gonna tell 'em what you said. I'm gonna—

*William enters the lobby.*

**JEFF** Hey.

**WILLIAM** Hey, Jeff.

*Pause.*

**DAWN** How you doin'?

**WILLIAM** I'm all right . . . What are you guys talking about?

*The elevator pings, off. Bill enters. Everyone turns and looks at him. He stops short.*

**BILL** What's goin' on?

**DAWN** Uh, nothin' too serious, Bill. I'm just doin' some police work right now. You can go back upstairs.

**BILL** What kind of police work?

**DAWN** Oh, well, it turns out while you're up there with "Jim," your buddy William here has been lyin' his ass off to the whole Police Department—!

| **BILL** | **JEFF** |
|---|---|
| What? | Hold on a second! |

**DAWN** —and gettin' away with it, because of you!

**WILLIAM** Excuse me?

**BILL** (*To William*) All right—whoa, whoa, wait a minute. (*To Dawn*) First of all, calm down—

**DAWN** You calm down.

**WILLIAM**   What did you just say?

**BILL**   Second of all—Just a second William—

**DAWN**   I don't have to calm down.

**BILL**   Second of all, what makes you say that?

**DAWN**   Because that's what he told *Jeff.*

*William and Bill look at Jeff. Pause.*

**JEFF**   Thanks a lot. That's great.

**DAWN**
And you just made a tremendous
jerk outta yourself with your
buddies on the detective squad
and the DA's office, and
tomorrow morning I am personally
goin' to the ADA myself and tell
him what a moron you are for
stickin' your nose in where it
doesn't belong and practically
getting the case thrown out. And
then everybody in the precinct
is gonna know what a lousy,
stupid, dishonest fuckin' cheat
you are. So tell 'em whatever you
want at my hearing, you mother-
fucking piece of *shit*. Because
after tomorrow nobody's gonna
believe a word you say about
me for the rest of your fuckin'
*life*!

**BILL**
That's what he told Jeff?



OK—OK—



OK, settle down!

Calm down!!!

*Dawn goes out onto the street and exits.*

**BILL** What is she talking about, Jeff?

*Jeff shakes his head.*

**BILL** (*To William*)   Somebody wanna tell me what she's talking about?

*William starts for the door.*

**BILL** Where do you think you're going?

*William walks out onto the street and off.*

**BILL** What the hell is going on?

*Jeff throws his newspaper in the trash can.*

# ACT TWO, SCENE TWO

*The next night. Jeff is alone in the lobby, asleep. Bill enters onto the street, carrying a bouquet of flowers. He looks at Jeff for a moment and then bangs on the door. Jeff wakes up, sees Bill, and hesitates. Finally he goes to the door, unlocks it, and steps back quickly.*

**BILL**   Hello, Jeff.

**JEFF**   Stay away from me.

**BILL**   Take it easy. I'm not gonna hurt you. You seen William?

**JEFF**   No.

**BILL**   He didn't come by yet?

**JEFF**   No. He's usually here by now.

**BILL**   All right, I'll just wait.

**JEFF**   (*Referring to the flowers*)   If those are for me, I don't want 'em.

**BILL**   Don't push me, Jeff. (*He sits down.*) So you know what they did to me this afternoon, thanks to you and your girlfriend?

**JEFF**   She's not *my* girlfriend.

**BILL**   They bumped me off the list for my gold shield. Seven years I been waiting to get on that list, and now I gotta wait another year at least. Or maybe two. Or maybe more, before I could get back on it. And maybe never. That's a loss for the community. OK? It's a personal loss to me, but it's a primary loss for the community, and I don't mind sayin' that. And all because that fuckin' bitch does not understand what it means to behave like a professional.

93

**JEFF**  Yeah . . . I'm sorry to hear about all that.

**BILL**  And you know what else she did?

**JEFF**  No.

**BILL**  She made a bitter enemy of every uniform cop in the city. She is ostracized in this Department as of now. Forever. Because maybe the brass'll get on my ass for making a little mistake, but the rest of the guys, they don't give two shits about that. What they care about is backing people up, sticking to your man, and not selling him out to the ADA because you think he's cheatin' on his wife with somebody else besides you. And OK, I got a little over-zealous and sometimes I put my two cents in where nobody's asking for it, but is that some kind of crime? I only do it 'cause I care. Yeah. I know that sounds corny, but I do. I care. I cared about William and what happened? All he had to do was tell me to mind my business, or anything like that, and I would have stayed out of it. But no. He's gotta abuse my confidence and with the help of my partner, the *sleuth,* he's gotta make me look like an asshole in front of the whole Goddamn division and every muckety-muck I been kissing the ass of for the last seven years. I mean I just can't believe it. I can't believe the sense of betrayal. I really can't.

**JEFF**  What happened to William?

**BILL**  What happened to William? He won't recant, that's what happened to William. His brother still says he wasn't there, and personally I believe him. They're gonna charge all three of 'em. And it's all thanks to you, Jeff.

**JEFF**  So now I gotta testify?

**BILL**  You're gonna testify, he's gonna testify, everybody's gonna testify. There's gonna be a lotta testifying.

**JEFF**  I never said I could testify. I just said I'd make a statement.

94

**BILL** Uh, yeah, they don't usually give you a choice. That's, like, the Law? You know: The Law? It has rules? Right and wrong? You're not allowed to break it?

**JEFF** The detectives said they thought he would recant.

**BILL** Well, I guess the detectives don't know everything. And I'll tell you something else, Jeff. I have a lot more respect for what he's doin' than I do for you. Because where I come from you stick up for your friends no matter what, and you don't sell 'em out for a piece of ass.

**JEFF** A piece of ass . . . !

**BILL** I'm sorry. I'm sure you had the highest noblest motives— I shouldn'ta said that.

**JEFF** I didn't do *any*thing for a piece of ass. . . . I didn't even *get* a piece of ass.

**BILL** You wanna know what I think?

**JEFF** No.

**BILL**
I think the both of youse are a coupla fuckin' rats as far as I'm concerned—Good for you! Now what time is he supposed to get here?

**JEFF**
I don't care what you think.

**JEFF** I don't know. Maybe he's not comin' tonight.

**BILL** All right. I can't hang around here all night. I have important police duties to perform. (*Heading for the elevators*) I'll be upstairs. Buzz me when he comes by.

**JEFF** Um, Bill? Sorry—She's not home.

**BILL** Who's not home?

**JEFF**  Mrs. Heinvald. I think she—

**BILL**  What do you mean she's not home?

**JEFF**  I was just gonna say, I think she went away for the weekend.

**BILL**  Oh yeah? And what makes you say that?

**JEFF**  Because about an hour ago she got in a big car with some guy and told me to have a good weekend.

**BILL**  What do you mean, "with some guy"? What'd he look like?

**JEFF**  I don't really like to talk about the tenants' personal business.

*Bill takes a step toward him.*

**JEFF**  All right, all right, take it easy—I don't know what he looks like, I didn't really see him.

**BILL**  Was he an older guy? Older guy?

**JEFF**  Could be. I didn't really notice, Bill.

**BILL**  All right . . . I know who it is. It's no big deal. All right . . . Always be honest with yourself, Jeff. It's the only way.

*Bill goes out of the lobby just as William enters onto the street. They both stop.*

**BILL**  Hello William.

**WILLIAM**  Hello Bill.

**BILL**  I been lookin' for you.

**WILLIAM**  Is this an official police inquiry?

**BILL**  Oh do me a favor . . . !

**WILLIAM**  Is this an official police inquiry?

**BILL**  No. Nothin' like that. But I love the arrogance. I really do. And after your brother goes to jail for the horrible thing he did, maybe you'll think about takin' it down a notch or two. Maybe. That's all I gotta say. Oh, and by the way, your boy in there's been sleepin' on the job.

*Bill exits. William takes a moment, then enters the lobby and crosses to Jeff.*

**WILLIAM**  Jeff, have you been sleeping on the job?

**JEFF**  No.

*William rips Jeff's badge off and grabs him like he's going to beat the shit out of him. Pause. He releases him.*

**WILLIAM**  You're fired. Now go get your stuff and get out.

**JEFF**  I'm sorry. (*William waves him away.*) I guess you don't want to hear what happened.

**WILLIAM**  I don't care, Jeff.

**JEFF**  Well—but—I mean, are you really firing me?

*William does not respond.*

**JEFF**  Because . . . I mean, are you really firing me because you think I've been sleeping on the job? Or because. . . Because it doesn't really seem like you are—since I don't know why you think that.

**WILLIAM**  Go home, Jeff.

**JEFF**  Well . . . I'd like to tell you what happened, if you want to hear about it.

**WILLIAM**  I *don't* want to hear about it, Jeff. I just want you to get your stuff and get out of here.

**JEFF**  Well . . . OK. But I'd still like to tell you what happened—

**WILLIAM**  I said get OUT of here, Jeff!

**JEFF**  All right.

*Silence.*

**JEFF**  Please don't fire me. I don't want to live with my brother anymore. I just put a deposit on an apartment *today*. Please don't fire me. (*Pause*) I know you think that I'm a frivolous person. But I didn't just lightly tell that lady cop what you said to me . . . no matter what you may think of me. I wouldn't do that. And I know what you're saying about the lawyer, which is a very serious problem—

**WILLIAM**  Jeff. You want to tell that little cop—You want to sit here and tell everybody in the world about everybody else because you don't have any life of your own, that's your own problem, but I don't want to hear about it.

**JEFF**  Well, I don't think that's what I was doing . . . I've thought about it and thought about it, and I don't think that's what I was doing . . . I was trying to do what I thought *you* woulda done, if it wasn't your brother.

**WILLIAM**  I wouldn't have done it behind my back.

**JEFF**  That's just the way it turned out. (*Pause*) But if you're firing me for sleeping on the job, then I think you should tell me why you think I was doing that. And if it doesn't have to do with anything to do with how I do my job, then I don't think you should be firing me.

**WILLIAM**  Well, Jeff, somebody *told* me they saw you sleeping on the job. Is that true?

*Pause.*

**JEFF**  No.

**WILLIAM**  It's not?

*Pause.*

**JEFF**  No.

*Pause.*

**WILLIAM**  All right. Pick up your badge.

**JEFF**  Pick up my—

**WILLIAM**  Pick up your badge. I shouldn't have hit you. I never should have confided in you in the first place. Pick up your badge now.

*Jeff picks up his badge.*

**JEFF**  I'd still like to tell you what happened, but thank you.

**WILLIAM**  Well, I'm not gonna fire you for something I didn't see you do, because I don't believe in that. I don't believe in that, and not you, or my brother, or those cops are ever gonna make me into the kind of person that believes in that. Now I don't want to talk about this anymore. I want you to pin that badge back on your shirt and sit back down behind that desk and try to do your job. And I don't care if you think it's all a joke. Because it's not a joke to me. I'm gonna finish up my rounds and then I'm going home. I have a lot of calls to make in the morning, and I gotta figure out what I'm gonna do next.

**JEFF**  Well . . . I just want to say, I really admire you.

**WILLIAM**  You admire me.

**JEFF** Yes.

*William exits. Jeff sits down at his desk and pins his badge back on his shirt. Pause. Dawn appears and enters. She is in her street clothes. She comes into the lobby.*

**DAWN** Hello. (*Pause*) I been waitin' across the street. (*Pause*) I didn't know if you'd be on.

**JEFF** I'm on.

**DAWN** (*Attempting a joke*)  Yeah, I see that ... (*Pause*) Well ... I just came by because I wanted to apologize for the way I handled everything last night ... I didn't mean to sacrifice your confidence—your confidentiality like that ... but I guess I really wanted to show him, and I guess I got a little carried away—

**JEFF** But are you gonna be able to patch things up with Bill OK? Because that's what I been concerned about.

**DAWN** Jeff, I'm really sorry—

**JEFF** But are things gonna be OK with you guys now? Because I been kind of worried about it—

**DAWN** Hey, Jeff, I came here to apologize: If you're gonna stand there and be an asshole about it why don't we just forget the whole thing?

**JEFF** Well, that is a really first-rate apology, I gotta hand it to you.

**DAWN** What do you want me to *say*!?

| **JEFF** | **DAWN** |
|---|---|
| I don't want you to say anything! I want you to get out of here, goddamn | All *right*! I didn't come outta this too |

it! Man, you are nothin'
but trouble!

well either, I want
you to know! My
career is probably
*over*!

**JEFF**  Yeah, good! Because you're a fucking *menace* and you oughta be stopped!

**DAWN**  Well, you're all gonna get your wish, so you can all just relax.

*Jeff does not respond.*

**DAWN**  Well, you obviously don't wanna talk to me right now, so—

**JEFF**  Right!

**DAWN**  —I'll just see you later.

**JEFF**  OK.

*Pause.*

**DAWN**  Well, they're changin' my tour, so I might not see you around too much. They're puttin' me on days for a while. So that'll be easier . . . Except no one'll work with me . . . Everyone's supposedly out to get me now. (*Pause*) I don't care. I didn't join the Police Force to make friends.

**JEFF**  Well . . . judging by how you've been handling yourself that's probably just as well.

**DAWN**  I don't care if people like me. I'm not just doin' this for my own amusement. (*Pause*) Jeff, I'm really sorry—

**JEFF**  Let's just forget it.

**DAWN**  OK. Thank you. (*Pause*) Did you get a date to your friend's wedding yet?

**JEFF**  No.

**DAWN**  Well, I'm still available. When is it, Saturday?

*Jeff does not respond.*

**DAWN**  Well . . . You probably wouldn't want to bring somebody who didn't know anybody . . . You know, with all your friends there . . .

**JEFF**  Yeah . . . You wouldn't really know anybody . . .

**DAWN**  Yeah, no, that's true . . . (*Pause*) So what are you gonna do now? You gonna stick it out here, or are you gonna . . . What are you gonna do?

**JEFF**  I don't know. (*Pause*) I was thinkin' about it . . . I was kind of hoping this whole experience would encourage me to rise to greater heights.

**DAWN**  What do you mean, like the advertising thing . . . ?

**JEFF**  Yeah. (*Pause*) I was trying to think what my old man would have done in this situation. Because for all his faults, my old man was not the kind of guy who sat around wringing his hands wondering what to do. So I was thinking about it today and I thought, if he was me he would have went right up to William and he would've said, "I'm givin' you twenty-four hours to go to the cops and tell 'em the truth, and then *I'm* gonna do it." And that's it. Bam. That's what he would have done. But then I thought, Yeah, but if it was one of his own who was in trouble, like one of his Navy buddies or something, he would have walked right in to those detectives and he would have lied his *ass* off. (*Pause*) I just don't want to be one of those pathetic guys in lobbies who are always telling you about their big plans to do some kind of shit you know Goddamn well they're never gonna do. I'd rather just be in the lobby and just *be* in the lobby. (*Pause*) To tell you the truth, sometimes I feel like I was worn out the minute I was born.

**DAWN**  But you shouldn't say that about yourself. I think you got a lot of potential. I think you're a great person. (*Pause*) I don't know, Jeff: How are you supposed to know if you're right and everybody else is wrong, or if you're just wreckin' your own chances?

**JEFF**  I wouldn't know. I never tried to do anything before.

*Long pause. Jeff hesitates, then reaches out tentatively and squeezes her shoulder.*

## THE END